Web Management with Microsoft® Visual SourceSafe™ 5.0

Web Management with Microsoft® Visual SourceSafe™ 5.0

Written by Steve Banick and Chris Denschikoff

Web Management with Microsoft Visual SourceSafe 5.0

Library of Congress Catalog No.: 97-67034

ISBN: 0-7897-1233-4

99 98 97   6 5 4 3 2 1

Interpretation of the printing code: the rightmost double-digit number is the year of the book's printing; the rightmost single-digit number, the number of the book's printing. For example, a printing code of 97-1 shows that the first printing of the book occurred in 1997.

Screen reproductions in this book were created using Collage Plus from Inner Media, Inc., Hollis, NH.

Credits

PRESIDENT
Roland Elgey

PUBLISHER
Stacy Hiquet

DIRECTOR OF MARKETING
Lynn E. Zingraf

PUBLISHING MANAGER
Jim Minatel

EDITORIAL SERVICES DIRECTOR
Elizabeth Keaffaber

ACQUISITIONS MANAGER
Cheryl D. Willoughby

ACQUISITIONS EDITOR
Jane K. Brownlow

PRODUCT DIRECTORS
Jácquelyn Mosley Eley
Benjamin Milstead

PRODUCTION EDITOR
Tonya Maddox

PRODUCT MARKETING MANAGER
Kristine Ankney

ASSISTANT PRODUCT MARKETING MANAGERS
Karen Hagen
Christy M. Miller

STRATEGIC MARKETING MANAGER
Barry Pruett

TECHNICAL EDITORS
Dr. Sunil Hazari
Matthew E. Brown

TECHNICAL SUPPORT SPECIALIST
Nadeem Muhammed

SOFTWARE SPECIALIST
Robin Sloan

ACQUISITIONS COORDINATOR
Jane K. Brownlow

SOFTWARE RELATIONS COORDINATOR
Susan D. Gallagher

EDITORIAL ASSISTANTS
Andrea Duvall

BOOK DESIGNER
Ruth Harvey

COVER DESIGNER
Ruth Harvey

PRODUCTION TEAM
Melissa Coffey
Terri Edwards
Tim Neville
Paul Wilson

INDEXER
Greg Pearson

Composed in *Century Old Style* and *Franklin Gothic* by Que Corporation.

About the Authors

Steve Banick, previously (and proudly) known as "the Network and Graphics Geek" in his past life as a corporate drone, has now found new life as a fledgling graphic designer. He still dabbles far too often in the technical area he claims to want to distance himself from. Principal of Steven Banick & Associates, he now works as a freelance designer for traditional and electronic media. Although he is married, he says he has dedicated his life to a greater purpose: to rid his house of the influence of cable television.

Chris Denschikoff has gotten away with being published for four years now. With documents as diverse as technical manuals, advertising copy, and interviews with rock and roll stars under his belt, he is hopefully up to the challenge of working for the Que publishing sweatshop. Currently, he writes for an Edmonton local Arts & Entertainment magazine, *SEE,* as well as does freelance work, such as the book you're holding. He also does design work in his spare time.

Acknowledgments

Steve's weird and wonderful thanks to:

Many thanks to my (sometimes less-than) understanding wife, Christina, for her grudging understanding and support for yet another reason to stare endlessly at my monitor. Additional thanks to my family and friends (who so kindly marveled at my new, "easy" job) who distracted me when I should have been writing. A shake of the fist at computer manufacturers who made me remember just how much happier I was before all of this "tech stuff" began. Finally, thanks to Errol for confirming my beliefs that I'm a bitter, petty, little man.

Chris remembers all the little people:

Thanks, Mrs. Putters, Grade 7 Language Arts was a wonderful start. Thanks to all my writerly friends who moved away and don't talk to me anymore: William, Chris, Jon, Tyler, Gareth, Rob, Carey, Steve, and yes, even Marge. Thanks, Mom, for that whole extended birth and labor thing; thanks, Dean, for the guitar to keep me sane(r); and thank you, Dad and Maureen, for four years of all our lives. And thanks to that bitter, petty, little man, Steven, and his very understanding wife Tina, for a place to live and all the beans a man can stand.

Steve and Chris extend thanks to:

Special thanks to our editors (past and present, even though our cheques are always late): Jane, Kelly, Tonya, Jácquie, Susan, Matt, Ben, and Stephanie. We're sure that if they saw us in person, they'd beat us with a whiffle bat. And thanks to everyone at that software start up that made us realize that we really were better than them. Having realized that and left, we're a whole lot happier now.

We'd Like to Hear from You!

As part of our continuing effort to produce books of the highest possible quality, Que would like to hear your comments. To stay competitive, we *really* want you, as a computer book reader and user, to let us know what you like or dislike most about this book or other Que products.

You can mail comments, ideas, or suggestions for improving future editions to the address below, or send us a fax at (317) 581-4663. For the online inclined, Macmillan Computer Publishing has a forum on CompuServe (type **GO QUEBOOKS** at any prompt) through which our staff and authors are available for questions and comments. The address of our Internet site is **http://www.quecorp.com** (World Wide Web).

In addition to exploring our forum, please feel free to contact me personally to discuss your opinions of this book: I'm **jeley@que.mcp.com** on the Internet.

Thanks in advance—your comments will help us to continue publishing the best books available on computer topics in today's market.

Jácquelyn Mosley Eley
Product Development Specialist
Que Corporation
201 W. 103rd Street
Indianapolis, Indiana 46290
USA

Contents at a Glance

Table of Contents

Introduction

Web sites are a headache. For both developers and users alike, they can be filled with a large number of files and links that may result in dead ends. For those creating and managing Web sites, it is a daunting task to ensure every file is up-to-date and accessible, and that there are no "wrong turns" leading to those dreaded dead ends. Because Web sites are made up of so many different file types, it is increasingly difficult to control the site's flow and guarantee its integrity. As more files are added in bigger and bigger sites, it is easier to have problems slip through the cracks, making maintenance a miserable chore.

Along with other vendors offering solutions for Web developers, Microsoft has promoted its product, Visual SourceSafe, as a means of stemming the tide. By providing a centralized tool for teams, Microsoft has empowered Web developers with the ability to directly monitor and control everything going into their Web site. This enables site managers to make sure what is going out to the public is of the best quality. When a Web site is the sum of its parts, developers want to make sure all of those parts work well. ■

Who Should Use This Book?

This book is intended for Web developers and site managers who are faced with swelling Web sites. If you are working with Web projects that are becoming increasingly difficult to manage, or if you want to ensure that all of your Web development work is conveniently organized, then this book will likely be of interest to you. In addition, as a developer taking advantage of the powerful team and version management facilities of SourceSafe, you will likely benefit from reading this book, which directly approaches three groups of people:

Web Developers

If you are in the trenches of Web development, busily coding and creating Web sites, then you are a Web developer. Therefore, you can benefit from the knowledge of versioning, content deployment, and library services. These three elements are of great importance if you are doing daily work on Web sites.

Project Leaders and Site Managers

If you are responsible for organizing or maintaining Web sites and teams of Web developers, then you are likely a project leader or site manager. As a project leader, you can benefit from the introduction of project security, project histories, reports, and journals. These features enable you to concentrate on the quality of the Web site you are managing. As a site manager responsible for the maintenance of the site and ensuring its safety, you will most likely benefit from SourceSafe's administrative facilities. Features such as shadow folders, backups, SourceSafe databases, and Web Projects all have a direct bearing on site managers.

Programmers

Although Web sites are increasingly being created and managed by non-programmers, trained programmers continue to play an important role in advanced Web interactivity. If you are working with server- or client-side extensions, software development for delivery on the World Wide Web, or developing interactivity to the Web site itself, then you are most likely a programmer. As a programmer, you are probably familiar with revision control systems, and can directly benefit from the library services, version tracking, and branches facilities of SourceSafe. These facilities enable you to group similar code and projects into unique versions while also enabling you to step back to a previous version at a moment's notice.

Why Use Visual SourceSafe?

With more software and tools required to complete the job every day, why would you want to saddle yourself with *another* tool? With more files to monitor and more people accessing those files, you need a centralized tool (in most environments) to maintain the data's integrity. As a site manager, you may have many sleepless nights due to your fears of losing changes or of problems resulting from change. Visual SourceSafe introduces stability and organization to an otherwise hectic and chaotic mix.

Before you decide that VSS is indeed "the tool for you," you should explore the advantages of a Revision Control System and VSS in particular. Read on—the bases are covered.

Revision Control Systems

Visual SourceSafe is Microsoft's current solution for the Revision Control System (RCS) market. An RCS is a concept familiar to many programmers. When programmers are working on a project, much like Web developers, they are often dealing with a large quantity of files and resources. The first job an RCS fulfills is organizing the many files into a useful set. From there, the programmer knows that all files associated with the project are included within that set, and new files can be added to the set. This reduces scrambling to find files that end up absent or were never added to the project. Second, the RCS provides "library services" for the project. When a file is being worked on, it is "checked out" by the library service for the duration of its editing. Once the editing is complete, the programmer returns the file to the RCS for safekeeping.

Each edit, or revision, can introduce unique changes and potential problems to the files. To allow a programmer to quickly correct problems introduced because of a revision, an RCS allows the programmer to step back to a previous version of the file that is stored within itself. Because of this safety feature, work on projects by multiple people can be done without fear of irreversible changes to files.

RCS packages apply easily to Web developers. When you are working on a file related to your Web site, you can safely edit that file. Once you have completed your editing, you sign the file into the revision control system for storage. When you or another developer need to modify the file, it is easily obtained from the library service. By monitoring and storing each change in the file, the RCS lets you make sure that a copy inside the RCS database is always up-to-date and functional. If future edits result in a file that is unusable, you can easily jump back to the last working copy and know who introduced the disastrous changes.

History of Visual SourceSafe

Microsoft Visual SourceSafe (VSS) grew out of developers' needs for a manageable RCS package. Prior to VSS, many developers used a product known as Microsoft Delta. Microsoft introduced VSS, which worked on a project basis, to address Delta's shortcomings. These shortcomings were based primarily on the command line interface, which provided no easy means for graphical integration. By using a project model, VSS provided a convenient means of project management in addition to the benefits of revision control. Initially targeted as a product for programmers, the advent of the World Wide Web introduced new possibilities for SourceSafe.

Because SourceSafe doesn't really care what is stored within its database, Web content can easily be managed using VSS, just as it could manage software code in the past. Microsoft's own Web development teams, as well as many other development houses, began to use VSS to coordinate and manage Web development teams and content. Realizing how VSS could be used by Web developers, Microsoft carried out slight enhancements to Visual SourceSafe version 4.0, and released version 5.0 with features specifically targeted for the Web developer.

SourceSafe 5.0 introduced several shortcuts and niceties to Web developers. Features such as Web Projects, link verification, site maps, and site deployment made the job easier for any developers currently using older versions of VSS for Web management. For new users, 5.0 offered direct support for Web content as opposed to previous versions' accidental implementation.

Visual SourceSafe versus Other Revision Control Systems

SourceSafe isn't the only game in town when it comes to RCS packages. However, it does offer several appealing options and features that other RCS programs cannot necessarily offer. Here are a few of SourceSafe 5.0's advantages:

- File relationships are managed in a project-oriented basis. Thus, you can spend less time managing projects and more time developing.
- Using shared components makes multiple projects possible. Through sharing, VSS maintains one stored version of a file that may appear in many projects.
- You can limit who can access and alter your Web site with the advanced security found in Visual SourceSafe.
- You can port Visual SourceSafe to just about any platform, be it Windows 3.1/NT/95, MacOS, or UNIX.
- Web Projects let you validate links in your Web pages, create comprehensive site maps, and easily deploy your site to your Web server.

■ You can integrate VSS with Microsoft FrontPage and Microsoft Visual InterDev for Web development.

■ A convenient and friendly graphical user interface (GUI), as well as a standard command line, make life much easier.

How This Book Is Organized

There has been a conscious effort to provide you with a clearly thought out and well organized reference book. You should find navigating easy and straightforward; its structure has been broken into five important sections, with appendixes following at the close of the book.

■ Part I, "Introducing Visual SourceSafe," provides you with a place to get your feet wet with VSS. Before you jump into anything more complex, you learn the essentials and how to get started. If you are new to Visual SourceSafe, the place you want to begin is Chapter 1, "Visual SourceSafe Concepts." Once you finish learning of VSS's basic innards, you can go on to Chapter 2, "Getting Started," which will take you to boot camp for revision control systems. If you want it all and want it now, head over to Chapter 3, "Visual SourceSafe Quickstart," for a super-fast, superficial treatment of VSS procedures.

■ Part II, "Using Visual SourceSafe," explores in more detail, using VSS for all of your daily work. Important project and file manipulation skills are introduced in this section, as well as the heady tasks of version management. Once you have grown more comfortable with VSS, the section you want to tackle is Chapter 4, "Visual SourceSafe Projects." When you're done mastering the project you can move onto Chapter 5, "File Basics," and learn more about files than you even think you want to know. After stuffing yourself with files, it's time for lighter fare with Chapter 6, "Deploying Content." After learning to publish a file anywhere VSS's tentacles can reach, you're ready for the big one—Chapter 7, "Version Management."

■ Part III, "Managing Projects with Visual SourceSafe," sets you up to shoulder the world using VSS. Specific information on managing large amounts of information and people, as well as backup issues, are introduced in these chapters. Once you're ready to start working large-scale with VSS, you will spend a great deal of time in these chapters. First you learn even more about projects in Chapter 8, "Controlling

Projects." After that, you should get everyone together to read Chapter 9, "Working in Teams." Then take some time out of your day to learn that it's always "safety first" with Visual SourceSafe by reading Chapter 10, "Backing Up Projects." Lastly, explore strange new worlds with Chapter 11, "Using Multiple Databases."

■ Part IV, "Exploring Advanced Topics," starts you into the real meat of advanced VSS. If you're hungry for power, it's past time you checked out Chapter 12, "Visual SourceSafe Administration." Those wanting to unite all of the battling development environments in their office should investigate Chapter 13, "Integration." If you like typing and aren't afraid to admit it, come on down to Chapter 14, "Command Line Tools," to learn about batch files. Do you think you paid too much for Visual SourceSafe? Learn all of the other neat programs you got when you bought VSS by reading Chapter 15, "SourceSafe Utilities." Lastly, promote computer harmony by reading Chapter 16, "Cross-Platform Usage."

■ Appendix A, "Batch Files and Command Line Options," provides you with a complete summary of the VSS Command Line tools' syntax, as well as sample batch files, which may prove of interest to you.

■ Appendix B, "Visual SourceSafe Options Summary," is a complete breakdown of all the options you can configure inside of either the Visual SourceSafe Explorer or Administrator.

Introducing Visual SourceSafe

Visual SourceSafe Concepts

The key to using Visual SourceSafe is understanding the ideas behind it. You can easily use the program and be ignorant of its inner workings, just as you don't actually need to understand the mechanisms of a car to operate one. In order to optimize your VSS experience you should understand the program's *how* and *why*. Just as an experienced mechanic immediately knows why his car has just started belching blue smoke, you, too, need a deeper understanding of Visual SourceSafe's inner workings; it's that much easier to troubleshoot things yourself when you know what's going on "under the hood." ■

Project management

Visual SourceSafe is a project-based system, which gives managers and developers alike a real appreciation for the aid it grants organization.

Transactions

Visual SourceSafe's quick and easy method of checking files in and out turns what is normally an unpleasant process into just another layer in your work pattern.

Keeping track of changes

Find the slackers on your development team with Visual SourceSafe's Orwellian History services.

Introducing an Example

In order to illustrate some principles in this book, an extended example of a fictitious company embarked on a nonexistent project is used. The company is named Site Corporati, and it specializes in corporate-level Web design solutions. It has captured a high-level client: the Fliedermaus Bank of Zurich. The Fliedermaus Bank of Zurich wants a corporate page to represent it on the Web, and it wants some simple Automated Teller Machine functionality from the site itself. The Site Corporati people will have their hands full, as the FBoZ is a demanding taskmaster, tolerating no mistakes and always wanting up-to-date reports. Not only that, but overseeing a Web development project with programming aspects is a daunting task. That's why Site Corporati's Project Leader, Jose, decided to try out Visual SourceSafe as a means of cutting down on mistakes and keeping track of progress.

Understanding Visual SourceSafe Projects

Other revision control systems are like one-night stands. You exchange phone numbers, promise to call each other next weekend, and then slowly forget. Not so with VSS—once you enter a file in the database, it's there for *good*. Not only is it there for good, but it's there in every form that the file may take while in the VSS database. Changes are logged and saved, allowing you to rollback to an earlier version at any time. The database itself doesn't get too bloated because Visual SourceSafe stores changes in a *reverse delta* format. This means that instead of saving a new copy of the file for every change you have made, VSS saves the change itself and then applies it to the original file. If you were to delete three lines of code from a file and then save it, the VSS database wouldn't save those lines as "gone." It would instead instruct the newest version to display the older version, minus those lines. The file system is an additive and subtractive one; instead of just replacing files, it modifies them to suit.

If you just went on, happily entering all these files into the VSS database, you would quickly have a mess on your hands comparable to Three-Mile Island—or a three-year-old's playroom. All these files need organization in some fashion or they are simply names in a database. This is where Projects come into play.

A Visual SourceSafe Project isn't like a project in other Microsoft development environments (such as Visual C++ or Visual Basic). It's more file-oriented and concerned with keeping your files *safe* as opposed to just keeping them all in one spot.

You must create a project to organize files in order for you to store files in Visual SourceSafe. The project itself is comparable to a file folder or directory on your hard drive; it stores files and their states, and it can contain other projects. It's important to note that you cannot directly modify a file in a project. Even though the project structure appears to mirror your hard drive, it is not a direct reflection. You can go through and delete all the files on your hard drive, but the organization in the VSS database will remain the same. In order to change a file within a project, you have to modify it outside of Visual SourceSafe and then reinsert it into the database.

FIG. 1.1
Visual SourceSafe protects your data from danger with three different layers.

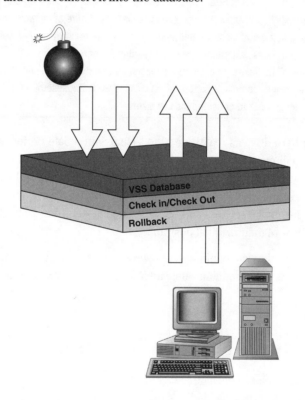

The project is an important concept to understand, because if you don't, you might otherwise simply insert all your files into the root project and complain that Visual Source-Safe doesn't offer adequate organization tools. A large burden is taken off a project manager's back because of the power of projects. By simply observing a project's contents, a user can ascertain what files are present, what files are currently checked out, and who checked out the absent files. The project also allows for a much cleaner organizational structure than other management systems that merely rearrange existing files. If the directory structure on your hard drive is convoluted and incomprehensible, you can clean it up by inserting files into a project in any fashion you want. Instead of embedding your images directory five directories deep, you can have it accessible directly from the *root* project. The root project is the equivalent to your root directory on a hard drive; all of the projects you create in VSS must be dependent upon it. Because the project exists as an organization and management tool, the torturous paths you've created do not affect the project because the files will never be executed.

Projects and Programming

Jeff is a project programmer at Site Corporati who is responsible for the Web project's underlying code functionality (CGI, Active Scripting, and so on). The nature of his work is such that he generates a large number of files. Normally, he keeps track of them by using a combination of hand-scribbled notes, his own memory, and misleading file names. With the Visual SourceSafe Project structure, all he has to do is insert his files in an orderly manner, and skip worrying about affecting the link/compile structure of his existing work. Because of all the saved time and effort, he can go back to criticizing his coworkers.

Think of your hard drive as reality, and the Visual SourceSafe Project system as virtual reality. The two dimensions are eerily alike, yet there are obvious differences. There are all sorts of things we don't like to deal with in the real world (jobs, bad directory structure, cold coffee) that we can't do much about. In the virtual world, we can reorganize them so that they make sense. Visual SourceSafe Projects' mentality allows you to sort things regardless of their original position.

All of this organization is meaningless, however, unless you are allowed some means of getting at those files you so laboriously added. Otherwise, VSS might as well be a glorified back-up system.

The Lowdown on Library Services

Files need organization. This simple fact has been handed down for generations—from the first Cro-Magnon who decided to keep track of rocks—to us, her proud descendants. The responsibility for this organization has largely fallen upon the shoulders of proto-librarians, as they're always messing about organizing things. This is why, when computers started taking over things, the natural analogy was that of a library.

Traditionally, entering a library is a neutral experience. On one hand, you have a large variety of interesting books at which to look, and some to take home. On the other hand, librarians are scary when it comes to fines, and you've got to be quiet about your rummaging. With Visual SourceSafe library services, you can take out as much as you want, not have to worry about returning things on time, and you can make as much noise as your workplace allows.

Checking Out Your Work

Like any good library, there's a means of checking files out of VSS. Unlike most libraries however, the means is an easy, fast, and relatively convenient one. Checking out a file is the process of informing the VSS database that you want to modify one of its files. The database, being coy, responds that it can't let you change the file itself, but it will loan you a working copy with which to play around. This working copy is stored in a working directory. Essentially, the working directory is a temporary folder into which you can jam all of your checked out files. The working directory can be some scratch disk somewhere, or it can be the original folder on your hard drive. Putting the working directory in a temporary directory places another barrier between you and the possibility of obliterating your original files.

A Designer's Perspective

Marge is the primary Web designer on the Site Corporati team. When she had to work on a file in the past, she did it *live*, or on the server. This became something of an embarrassment, however, because it was always apparent to the casual browser that someone was doing work on the site. ("Under Construction" signs just don't cut it anymore.) With Visual SourceSafe she can integrate changes at her own pace, and then implement them immediately. If she makes a grave mistake, she can rollback just as easily.

Most importantly, though, is the fact that through check in and check out she can keep track of her work and not worry about making dangerous or experimental changes, because there's always a backup copy in the Visual SourceSafe database.

Checking In Your Work

Again like any good library, you can also check files back in. Unlike most libraries, however, there's no sense of lingering guilt when checking in late files. After checking in the file you've modified, it becomes the current copy. If you go back to check that file out again, it'll be the version you had just checked in. The entire check in process lets you stop errors before they happen. If you realize you've introduced an error or incontrovertibly screwed up a file, you don't have to check it back in. You can simply change the course of history and undo the check out, as if it never occurred. This forces Visual SourceSafe to use the copy that it has stored internally and ignore any changes you may have made since the last check out. Unfortunately, you can't erase the fact that you were the one to incontrovertibly mess up a file in the first place. Check in allows you to go over your work in a safe area (the working directory) without being concerned whether you can save changes or not. When you're finished, you can go over the file that one last time, and then check it in.

Your files get checked in, and you feel a wonderful freedom. All of your changes are made, saved, and now permanently protected by Visual SourceSafe. The job isn't done yet, though, because even if you have the final version of your file, it does you no good if no one can look at it. In the example of a Web site, you've finished editing the Index.HTM and now want it to go on your server. In order to do this, you have to publish the file using the Get command.

Publishing to a Remote Server with *Get*

Get is to check in and check out what publishing a book is to editing and proofreading. Sure, you can publish a book without the latter two, but it sure doesn't read well. Get is the same way, as it is the culmination of your checking in/editing/checking out process. Basically, the command moves a copy of the most current version of the file to a location you specify. This copy is ostensibly to be used or viewed by others who don't have access to the Visual SourceSafe project. However, Get can also be used to simply place copies of a file somewhere, as it's a copy command all dressed up in publisher's clothing.

The first layer of Visual SourceSafe file protection stems from the fact that it maintains a separate copy of your files instead of keeping track of existing files on your hard drive. The second layer comes from the fact that you can't modify those files directly, and instead have to check out files, leaving the original untouched until you feel the modified file is ready to be checked back in. The third layer protecting you is within the Get command; you decide when and where your files become live, a procedure of vital importance when it comes to displaying time-sensitive Web information. The fourth layer is that you can easily revise, or even totally roll back any of your changes to a file using the History services.

The Importance of History Services

The concept of the history of a file is a new one to the casual user, yet it's been adopted by most of the revision control systems out there. The problem with previous incarnations of the History function is that you had to navigate strange, text-based menus, or were only able to roll back one version. One of Visual SourceSafe's advantages over its hairier, uncouth predecessors is the fact that its History function is both easily accessible and understood, thanks to VSS Explorer's graphical interface.

The unthinkable happens: you've created, checked out, checked in, and published a file to your live server. Unfortunately, on your last check in, you let a fatal error slip into the file, and then compounded things by later checking out the file and checking it back in, with the error still present. You can't use the Undo Check Out, because the error was introduced two versions ago. What you need is access to the file's history.

Visual SourceSafe tracks files on a change-by-change basis; the program has several different versions of any one file in its database. This is known as its *history*. In the example crisis just narrated, you could easily call up the file's history, choose the version of the file you know is correct, then roll back to an earlier version. This makes history a valuable tool for correcting errors; its applications, however, can be much larger.

History allows you to track usage and changes within the file. From a managerial point of view, this is invaluable. You can determine who has accessed the file how many times, and more importantly, how many changes they made. In the case of an ever-evolving project, you can track down what changes occurred when, in order to determine what changes were the beginning of a new paradigm, and which were creeping featuritis.

Using the Differences Service

So you've looked at your files' histories, but you're dealing with a monster of a Web site, with some files containing thousands of lines of code. There's no way you have the time or inclination to pore over every line, trying to detect what has changed between version nine and version ten. What you need is some method of displaying the differences between those two versions.

Managing Data

Jose is the project leader for Site Corporati. He is in charge of making sure the programmers and designers see eye to eye, and more importantly, making sure that the Fliedermaus Bank of Zurich is kept up-to-date on its Web project's status. He can use Visual SourceSafe as a means of project tracking and to ensure that his coworkers don't waste too much time because of errors.

When you look at a file's differences, you are comparing the file to a different incarnation of itself, or to another file entirely. Differences make it visually clear what lines have been added, deleted, or changed between the two files. You select a file, and then a different version of that file, and compare them. The two files are displayed side-by-side, with the changes highlighted. This is an invaluable tool when it comes to trying to find out what suddenly made an HTML file stop working properly between versions. The Differences function can only display two files side-by-side at any one time.

The Importance of Commenting

Another aspect of history is its ability to comment files as you process them. On the eve of every check in/check out/Get is the prospect of entering a descriptive comment. Commenting your files is much like commenting your code—both are something you should always do. When tracing back versions of a file, it's much easier to read the comment "added header graphic" than it is to examine the code to find in which version you added the header graphic. It's also invaluable for people not familiar with the project, as it allows them to extrapolate what purposes a file could have that aren't immediately apparent from the file name.

Using Comments as a Roadmap

Jose had used up some vacation time in the Hawaiian Islands just before the Fliedermaus Bank of Zurich project started. When he came back, the rest of the Site Corporati team was already two weeks into the project. He needed to familiarize himself with the project and its trappings quickly. Luckily, both Marge and Jeff are of the anal-retentive school of programming, and comment their Visual SourceSafe check in and check out processes religiously. Because of this, Jose is easily brought up to speed on the project's progress, and can actually make accurate reports to marketing. The only negative outcome of his vacation was a bad sunburn.

Getting Online with Web Projects

The Get command is a valuable one, as it allows you to publish from the Visual SourceSafe database from inside a graphical interface without all the fun of hunting down each directory of your actual project. However, it has one strict limitation—it cannot publish to remote servers. This is a pretty big flaw, since most Web developers are not doing their work from the actual computer on which the site will be published. In the old days you had to rely on File Transfer Protocol to get the site content to its eventual home on the computer. You still use FTP during your use of VSS, but at least you get to hang out in the cool graphical interface while you're about it.

In order for your project to be considered a Web Project, it has to be defined as such by the Visual SourceSafe Administrator. If your project has been defined as a Web Project, you can use the Deploy command to publish on far-off and exotic servers. You still have to use a separate delivery medium such as FTP, but you can do so from the comfort of the Visual SourceSafe graphical interface. VSS knows that a Web Project should be published outside of your local computer, so it will accept an URL as a destination. Web Projects can also use some of VSS's Web-specific functions such as link verification and automatic site map generation.

Link verification is the process of testing all the links within your Web Project to ensure that they lead to relevant files and addresses. This is an important diagnostic tool to run over a site just before it's ready for "prime time." In the old days, testing links was done by the simple expedient of going through every link by hand, ensuring that it went some-where. This sort of innovation will win over even the Luddite Web developers out there.

The site map is helpful because it allows you to keep track of large and complex sites' organization. Not only does it help you keep track, but it also gives you a document that you can show other people. One of the largest concerns with Web site development is justifying and explaining the site's organizational scheme to outsiders. With a site map in hand, you can quickly and efficiently bring them up-to-date.

From Here...

Chapter 3, "Visual SourceSafe Quickstart," helps you put your hard-earned concepts to the test with a rapid run-through of basic Visual SourceSafe functionality.

Chapter 8, "Controlling Projects," teaches you how to steer a straying project back onto the right path using VSS's comprehensive project management tools.

Chapter 12, "Visual SourceSafe Administration," enables you to become enlightened with the knowledge that there's more to Visual SourceSafe than just being a user. Find out how to enable two people to work on the same file, and set guidelines and permissions for your users to ensure no one works on the wrong files.

CHAPTER 2

Getting Started

So, you've read the introduction and the concepts. You think Microsoft Visual SourceSafe is the cure for what ails you. Where do you start? Think of this chapter as your helpful little guide to getting up-to-speed on Visual SourceSafe before you strike off on your own into the following chapters. Tighten your seat belt and put on your favorite music because this chapter will fly by fast! ■

The many faces of SourceSafe

Visual SourceSafe isn't just one tool—it is actually a small suite of tools that enhances your productivity. It is important for you to know which tool does what, and when you should use it.

Get moving with SourceSafe

Just because you've opened the box doesn't mean you're done. Once you've installed that software, you need to get it ready to work.

Visual SourceSafe Components

When you think of a program such as Microsoft Word, you think of only one face. You load a program when you need to use it, close it when you're done. Visual SourceSafe doesn't behave in this traditional form—instead, VSS is a tertiary set of tools available for your use when working with your primary development tools. It is important for you to know exactly what tools VSS provides you, and when you should step up to the plate and use them. This is what you accomplish now, so get comfortable.

VSS Administrator

The Visual SourceSafe Administrator is the keen-eyed traffic cop, perched at the corner, monitoring behavior and enforcing the law when necessary. When you are working with VSS, the Administrator program is your front end to controlling SourceSafe's behavior. The primary job that you perform with the Administrator is handling your VSS installation's security aspects. Adding and removing users, setting permissions on projects, controlling databases: all short work in the VSS Administrator, as shown in Figure 2.1.

FIG. 2.1

Exercise your urge for power trips with the VSS Administrator. Add and remove users, set permissions, even dictate your team's file types. Now that's control!

The VSS Administrator is limited to (surprisingly enough) administrative tasks for SourceSafe. You do not carry out your everyday development work inside the Administrator; instead, you use the VSS Explorer. The Administrator has none of the Explorer's functionality; the only purposes the Administrator serves are to organize users and set permissions.

The Project Manager and VSS Administrator

Jose, the project manager, is responsible for monitoring and maintaining the production staff at Site Corporati. Each time a new developer joins the team or an old one leaves for greener pastures, it's Jose's job to make sure he or she is in or out of the VSS system. The VSS Administrator is the tool that Jose uses most often for managing the development team's production process.

Because Site Corporati's staff is not limited to those working on the Bank of Zurich project, Jose has wisely chosen to limit only the development team access to the project files. Why risk problems? It's easier for Jose to set up project permissions than to try to fix a disaster later. Besides, the team assigned to the Bank of Zurich has always had a nasty competition going with the team assigned to the FrankenWeiner project.

Visual SourceSafe Explorer

The heart of almost all interactions with VSS happens with the VSS Explorer. In your day-to-day development work, you use this tool to manipulate your files and projects in a convenient graphical user interface. All this, and a pretty face too! The VSS Explorer is used when you are taking advantage of SourceSafe's library services and version management and do not wish to use a command line tool; VSS Explorer is also used when you are not working in an integrated environment. Your interaction with files and projects inside Explorer is through pull-down menus, the toolbar, command-key sequences, and right-clicking items. The vast majority of this book's VSS operations discussions involve the VSS Explorer. Take a look at it in Figure 2.2.

FIG. 2.2

The VSS Explorer: Get used to it, it's going to become your friend. The SourceSafe Explorer is the predominant fixture for all VSS operations, including library services.

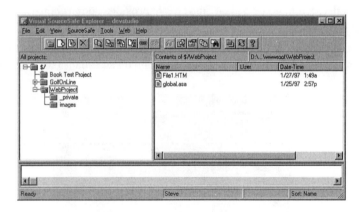

If you are working in a development environment, you may want to directly call upon the features of VSS without ever having to leave. Although some development environments offer integration with VSS(), many environments rely on the ability to launch external commands and *batch files*. This is where Command Line tools come into play.

▶ **See** Chapter 13, "Integration," on **p. 175** for more information about integration.

The Web Developer and VSS Explorer

Marge dislikes tools. She sees them as interruptions to her Zen-like design "flow." All the same, she chooses to use the VSS Explorer, rather than Command Line tools, for her work with VSS. When she has the chance, she takes advantage of VSS integration in a few development tools, but on the whole, she relies on the Explorer's Graphical User Interface (GUI) to maintain her files. Because the Command Line tools are an all-text and somewhat counter-intuitive interface, they are definitely un-Marge.

By using VSS's project-oriented layout, Marge has been smitten with the organizational abilities of the Explorer's GUI. She religiously splits her work into appropriate and nested subprojects. Often the thorn in Jose's back, Marge likes to exercise her individuality by setting up her own file types to extend her organizational structure. Although it's much to Jose's chagrin, it allows Marge a lot of flexibility in her work.

Command Line Tools

Are you a DOS hound? A "command line until you die" sort of guy or girl? On the other hand, do you just have the need for automated scripts or batch files for your frequently needed VSS functions? Visual SourceSafe provides comprehensive command line tools that allow you to control exactly what goes where, without worrying about a graphical user interface. The VSS Command Line tools are usually the quickest way of carrying out actions with VSS—if you know exactly what you are doing (see Figure 2.3).

FIG. 2.3

Just because you use Windows doesn't mean you can't be cryptic. The VSS Command Line tools allow maximum control over actions, and provide a means for scripting sequences.

Using the VSS Command Line tools allows you to write specialized scripts, or batch files, which you can call from a development environment. If you find that using the VSS Explorer slows you down, but your environment does not support VSS directly, then this is your best choice.

The Programmer and the Command Line

Sure, Jeff could use the integration of VSS in Visual C++ and the other environments he uses, but where would the fun be in that? Jeff, a throwback from the DOS days, fancies himself a UNIX and command line kind of guy. Under these pretenses, he chooses to do the majority of his work using the VSS Command Line.

After spending a few hours writing batch files of his frequently used tasks, Jeff can now spend mere moments manipulating his source code so he has more time to pat himself on the back for his brilliance. All this, and without using an effete GUI any more than he has to.

Setting Up Visual SourceSafe for the First Time

Ready to head into the world of VSS? Pull out your CD-ROM and pull up a chair. You can set yourself up with VSS in three easy steps:

1. Select one machine to act as the SourceSafe server and install the software to create the initial database for VSS. This may be your main workstation, or it may be a file server.

2. If you are using VSS on more than one machine, install VSS on any workstations you need.

3. Use the VSS Administrator to set up your initial security settings, including users and permissions.

Installing SourceSafe on the Server

Carrying out an installation on your server is a simple task. Follow these steps:

1. Insert the Visual SourceSafe CD-ROM (or other media) into your server's drive.

2. If you are using Windows NT 4.0 or Windows 95, go to the Start menu and choose Run. If you are using Windows NT 3.51, choose File, Run from the Program Manager.

3. Type the path to the VSS Setup program. This is usually *<the letter of your CD drive>*:\ setup.exe, followed by hitting the Enter key.

N O T E Keep in mind that if you encounter any difficulties or unanswered questions during the installation, you should refer to the Microsoft documentation included with your software. ▪

As you progress through the Setup program you are to provide your license information (your name isn't just there for posterity) and agree to the end-user license agreement. With that out of the way, you have to take a stand and choose the type of installation you need, as shown in Figure 2.4.

FIG. 2.4

Three choices shouldn't cramp your style too much. These options from the Setup program allow you to choose the type of installation you need. Don't waffle, dig in!

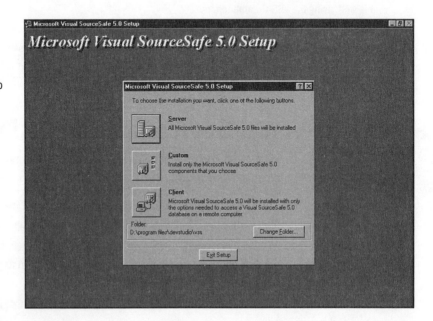

This dialog lists the three most common installation types for Visual SourceSafe. The options are:

- Server. For stand-alone VSS machines and your central database server, this is the preferable option. In choosing this you give the order to install everything you need in order to use Visual SourceSafe. This includes the SourceSafe client programs (SourceSafe Explorer and Administrator), several utilities, and the help files. The most important aspect of this option is the creation of a blank SourceSafe database, ready to store your work.

- Custom. If you are looking to fine-tune your Visual SourceSafe installation, this is the option for you. Not every one of your installations will need a database, though it may need other options. You can use the Custom installation to make your SourceSafe installation something you can write home to momma about.

- Client. With some of your workstations only needing to interact with an existing database, it's best to keep the installation to a minimum. Choosing the Client installation drills Setup into depositing only the client programs and help files without the extra fuss.

To begin, you only need to click your choice from the list to begin the installation. With this being your first installation, odds dictate your mouse is wavering over the Server option. To install your server, follow these steps:

1. Confirm that the destination folder is the correct path. You can change the path by clicking the Change Folder button.

2. Click the Server button. This starts the installation process.

3. Once the installation is complete and you've finished reading the Microsoft feel-good propaganda, you are told the installation is complete. Click the OK button to dismiss the dialog box and close the Setup program.

Your server installation is done! The nice thing about Visual SourceSafe's Setup program is that it's forgiving. In fact, it will even forgive you when you forget your anniversary. When you choose an installation method from the Setup program, you aren't locked into it for the rest of your Web management life. You can easily run the Setup program again after your installation to fine-tune your masterpiece and reaffirm your SourceSafe-enriched existence.

Setting Up Clients on the Network

Not content to work in VSS all by your lonesome? Rightfully so—everything is better in a group. Each workstation that you set up on your network to access the central VSS database only requires the client software; they do not need any server components. On each client machine, launch the Setup program (from either a network installation point or your distribution media) and enter headlong into the Setup program again.

▶ **See** Chapter 11, "Using Multiple Databases from Visual SourceSafe Explorer," on **p. 147** for more information about multiple databases.

Because you do not need to install server components, you should select Client, the third pretty icon in the Setup options. This option will install only the VSS Client software and help files, including the VSS Books Online (which aren't nearly as invaluable as this book, of course).

N O T E An important note about client installations involving integration with a development environment: By default, the VSS Setup program does not install the required files to use VSS within environments such as Visual C++, Visual InterDev, and the like. If you need integration support, you must choose a Custom installation and specifically select integration support for installation. If you have already installed VSS and find that you need integration, you can later add the option by launching the Setup program and choosing to Add/Remove components of your installation. This process is identical to customizing your installation and lets you fiddle with your installation at your convenience. ■

Part

I

Ch

2

Customizing Your Installation

Not a traditional person? Standard installations got you down? Aware that not every installation is created equal, the VSS Setup lets you pick and choose exactly what you want to install. If you are doing a new installation from scratch, you can select Custom, the second pretty icon from the Setup program. This provides you with a screen of components from which to choose for installation. If you have already installed VSS and are looking to add or remove components from your installation, you can run the VSS Setup program to achieve the same result. This screen is shown in Figure 2.5.

N O T E You can use the Setup program to refine your current installation. When you launch the Setup program it quickly determines what components you have installed. You are given the choice to add or remove components from your installation, to reinstall Visual SourceSafe with the current components, or to remove SourceSafe from your system. The process of adding and removing components is identical to customizing your initial installation. ■

FIG. 2.5
The Custom installation option lets you choose exactly when you want to install. Visual C++ and Visual InterDev users will want to take note of the option to Enable SourceSafe Integration.

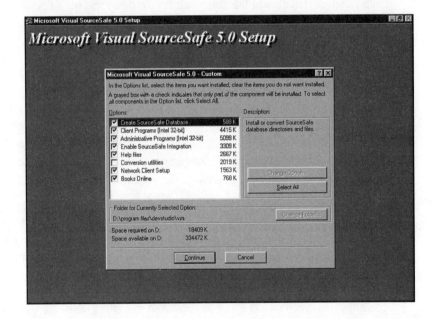

Each check box in the Custom installation screen represents a specific component of Visual SourceSafe:

- Create SourceSafe Database. This option tells the Setup program to create a bare, basic VSS database on the target machine. You need to select this option if you are using this machine as a server.

- Client Programs. The real "programs" of Visual SourceSafe are the VSS Explorer and Command Line tools. This option installs the programs specific to your platform (that is, if you're using an Intel processor, the Intel programs are installed).

- Administrative Programs. The VSS Administrator, as you learned before, enables you to manage your VSS installation. This option installs the program for your platform.

- Enable SourceSafe Integration. If you are using a development environment that takes advantage of SourceSafe integration, you must choose this option to install the required components. This option is required if you are using Microsoft Visual C++, Visual InterDev, and most other Microsoft development products.

- Help files. The online help for both Visual SourceSafe Explorer and Administrator are installed with this option. You have the option to install one or the other.

- Conversion utilities. If you previously used another RCS package, such as PVCS or Delta, you should install this option to convert your existing data to Visual SourceSafe.

- Network Client Setup. Do you have other machines on the network you need to set up with VSS? You can install this option to create a network installation point for future installations. This enables you to install directly from the network rather than using your distribution media for each installation.

- Books Online. The Microsoft VSS online reference manual, which contains the answer to just about every question you could imagine, and a lot you couldn't.

Remember, if you choose not to install an option at this time, but decide you need it later, you can go back and add it by running the Setup program. Alternatively, if you need to remove an option you have installed you can always do that, too.

Making VSS Available on the Network

Having a VSS database on your server doesn't do you any good if no one else on your network can see it. Thankfully, making the database accessible by users on your network is a trivial task if you're familiar with Windows networking. If you're not familiar with Windows networking and resource sharing, well, shame on you. You can refer to the documentation included with your operating system, which is presumed to be Microsoft Windows-based.

Deep in your server's hard drive, the VSS installation directory contains several key files that tell clients who can access what and where it can be accessed. Using Windows networking, you must *share* the VSS directory as a network resource. This lets other machines and VSS users access your VSS database by using a standard Windows *Universal*

Naming Convention directory path on the network (such as "\\Server\VSS") if you had shared the VSS directory as "VSS." You can select a VSS database to connect with from within the VSS Explorer.

Setting Up Your First User

Once you have shared your database, it is available to all users on the network depending on how you've set access. All security within VSS itself is handled on a user/project basis. Before you can begin working with VSS, you have to create a user with which to connect the database. To do this, you must launch the VSS Administrator for the first time.

▶ **See** Chapter 12, "Visual SourceSafe Administration," on **p. 153** for more information about security.

When you run the VSS Administrator for the first time, it will greet you with a dialog box asking for a password, as shown in Figure 2.6. Because this is the first time you have entered the program, the password is blank and you shouldn't see this dialog box. If you do, just hit the Enter key or click the OK button to continue.

FIG. 2.6

Halt! Who goes there? The VSS Administrator asks you to confirm who you are by demanding a password to enter. Type it in and press Enter.

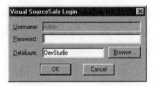

Now it's time to get down to business. Adding your first user is a simple task, one that you'll no doubt finish in record time by following these simple instructions:

1. Choose User, Add User. This opens the Add User dialog box, shown in Figure 2.7.

2. In the top box, Username, enter the username for the person for whom this VSS account is being set up.

NOTE Usually your VSS username is the same as your Windows networking username, to allow for automatic logins to VSS. If you choose a different username, you are prompted for a username and password each time you start the VSS Explorer. ▪

3. In the bottom box, Password, enter the password for the person who will be using the account. Remember that passwords are case-sensitive. You may even choose not to use a password at all.

4. Click the OK button.

FIG. 2.7
Not much to it, is
there? The Add User
dialog box has that
minimalist feel. Here
you can provide a
username and a
password.

Voilà! Your user is now in SourceSafe, as shown in Figure 2.8. You can get down to work.

FIG. 2.8
Your name in lights!
Well, not exactly—but
all the same, your new
user has been added
and is ready for use.

From Here...

Now that your Visual SourceSafe installation is ready to go, here are important chapters to move on to:

- Chapter 3, "Visual SourceSafe Quickstart," steps you lightly into the VSS Explorer to familiarize you and work hands-on with the tool.

- Chapter 4, "Visual SourceSafe Projects," begins your more comprehensive exploration of VSS and working with it for your Web development.

- Chapter 12, "Visual SourceSafe Administration," explores, in detail, the tasks of managing your VSS installation and securing your data.

CHAPTER 3

Visual SourceSafe Quickstart

Some of you computer users out there are too impatient to read a book fully even though you've paid the full price for it. That's why the Quickstart chapter immediately follows the basic concepts chapter. Here you learn how to do many of the things possible in SourceSafe, albeit in an abbreviated fashion. You also learn some basic commands in the SourceSafe library, which will tantalize you into learning more. ■

Exploring the Explorer

Here's a brief breakdown on the functionality of Visual SourceSafe's graphical user interface, the Explorer.

Create projects fast

In a real hurry? This quick start section on creating projects will get you started faster than you can say "jackrabbit."

Keeping track of your files

Get on the fast track to managing your content using Visual SourceSafe.

Inside the Explorer

Before you can start anything, you need to understand the SourceSafe Explorer. This is the graphical user interface in which you do the majority of your work. The setup is quite simple, and adheres to "windows" truisms such as panes, adjustable borders, and the drop-down menu. There are five major segments to the Visual SourceSafe Explorer, as shown in Figure 3.1.

FIG. 3.1
The Visual SourceSafe Explorer allows access to a variety of commands from either the toolbar or the pull-down menu.

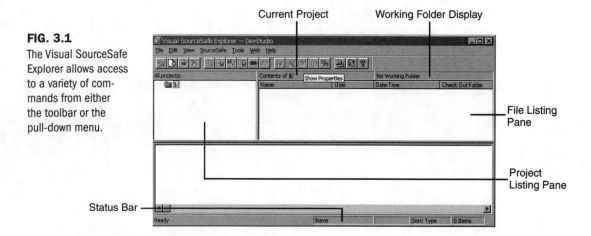

The first and topmost is the ubiquitous menu bar. This is followed immediately by the icon-rich toolbar, containing most of the everyday commands you need in order to use SourceSafe.

Below both of these come the Project and File panes. In the left is the Project listing, containing the goods on all of your projects. If you've just started, it should be empty of projects. On the right side is the File listing. This pane contains all of the files that are contained within whatever Project is selected in the Project listing. Once again, if you're just starting out, it, too, should be empty. By right-clicking a project you can duplicate many of the commands found in the menu bar. This also applies to File listings, although the command subset available will obviously be different.

The current project and working folder paths are displayed above the File listing, but below the task bar. If you are ever unsure of your location, you can view this area to regain your bearings. The status bar runs along the bottom; it contains information pertinent to whatever process you are currently enacting. if, for example, you are checking in a file, the status bar will say so. It will also display what file you are checking in and to where.

Creating Your First Project

Everyone remembers his or her first time, and you'll be no exception. The things you'll remember, though, are the ease of use and safety that Visual SourceSafe grants your files. SourceSafe is organized around a Project hierarchy, so the first thing you need to do is create a project in which to store your soon-to-be-protected files.

1. Choose File, Create Project.
2. Give your project a descriptive name and comment to make it easier to keep track of (see Figure 3.2).
3. Click OK.

FIG. 3.2
A logical and organized titling system can be invaluable for internally tracking projects.

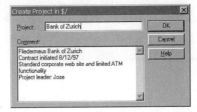

The new project is there, sparkling and pristine, an empty vessel waiting to be filled. Remember to create your projects intelligently. You can split up projects in ways that would never work on your hard drive, but make perfect sense in Visual SourceSafe. It's important to put the right files into the right projects to avoid duplication and confusion. Luckily, adding files is an easy process, as illustrated in Figure 3.3.

1. Select the project into which the files will be going.
2. Choose File, Add Files.
3. Enter either a directory path or browse to your files' locations.

FIG. 3.3
You can add multiple files, or files of multiple type, from the Add Files dialog.

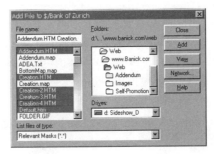

4. Click OK to add the files.

5. Comment your files, preferably with the date so you know when you included them.

6. If you have more files to add, repeat Steps 1–4. If you're finished adding, click Close to end the Add File process.

You should now have a project in the left-hand Project Listing window, and at least one entry in the right-hand File Listing window (see Figure 3.4). Now that you've managed to insert a project and some files, it's time to see how you can manage them to your benefit.

FIG. 3.4
The fruits of your labors—a new project with accompanying file listing.

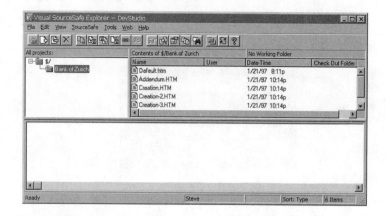

> **N O T E** To access most of the commands found in the task- or menu bars, you can right-click either a project or file listing. What commands are displayed and which are grayed out as unavailable will give you a better understanding of what is possible from each listing. ■

Managing Content Files

There comes a time in any users' life when they have to admit they're accumulating data for the simple reason of having it. Usually at that time they're forced to either use some of that data, or delete it entirely. If you're lucky and have installed Visual SourceSafe, you can get through your midlife crisis by using its project management tools. Assuming you've already created a project and added files to it, the next logical step is to check out files so you can work on them. Refer to Figure 3.5 for an insider's view:

1. Highlight either a file or project from its respective listing by clicking that file or project.

2. Select SourceSafe, Check Out.

3. If you haven't already, you'll be asked to define a working directory.

4. A copy of the file/project will be automatically moved to your working directory. Checked out files will be limned in red in the SourceSafe Explorer.

FIG. 3.5
Visual SourceSafe does not allow you to check out files without defining a working folder.

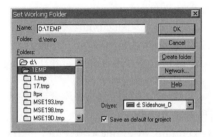

 Visual SourceSafe file selection tips:

1. When selecting files, the standard Windows convention of control-click or shift-click to select multiple files holds true.

2. When searching for files within a project, you can do wild card or status searches from the View, Search menu on the menu bar.

3. While not really a selection tip, you can also make finding files easier by using the View, Sort command on the menu bar.

Check out time came and went, and now it's time to restore your carefully edited gems to the hoard. To do so you need a breakdown on the check in process, which you can see in Figure 3.6.

FIG. 3.6
Insightful comments during the check in phase can remove confusion later on, when attempting to discern what changes were made when.

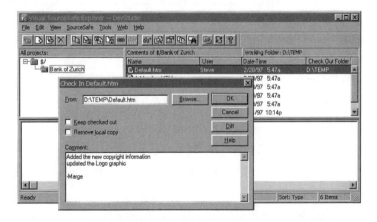

Part
I

Ch
3

1. Select a file or project to return to the Visual SourceSafe database.
2. Choose SourceSafe, Check In.
3. Comment your file accordingly and click OK to check the file in.

Sometimes you want a file to end up somewhere other than where it was saved. Instead of copying it or saving it in another program, Visual SourceSafe has the Get command to put files in their place. This is usually a live directory where others can access the final copies of your work. You can get files by following these steps and studying Figure 3.7:

1. Select the files or projects to be published.
2. Choose SourceSafe, Get Latest Version.
3. Specify where the file is to end up, by either a directory path or browsing.
4. Click OK.

FIG. 3.7
Getting a file allows you to publish multiple copies without too much fuss or bother.

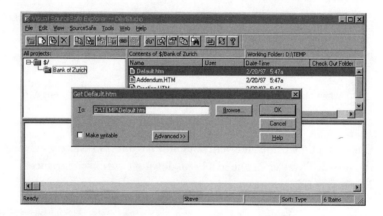

In case of mistakes, there are two quick fixes to be applied. The first, in the case of an erroneous check out, is the undocheckout function:

1. Select the file or project to be corrected.
2. Choose SourceSafe, Undo Check Out.

Secondly, in the case of a file that was added to a project when it shouldn't have been, there's the simple expedient of deleting it, as illustrated in Figure 3.8.

1. Select the file or project to be removed from the SourceSafe database.
2. Choose File, Delete.
3. In the dialog that appears you can check a Destroy Permanently box. This removes any chance of undoing the delete process.
4. A dialog box appears, double-checking that you want to delete the file(s). Click OK.

FIG. 3.8
Files that are deleted from a project can be recovered because they are still in the Visual SourceSafe database. Files that have been destroyed are no longer in the database and cannot be recovered.

This Quickstart is intended to get you off the ground when it comes to various Visual SourceSafe functions, and is by no means intended to be a complete tutorial. Now that you have a basic grasp of Visual SourceSafe, you will be better able to understand how the program can help you revise and protect your files.

Part
I

Ch
3

From Here...

For the extended concepts that are the roots of these processes investigate:

Chapter 5, "File Basics," covers all of the file commands that are possible with Visual SourceSafe.

Chapter 6, "Deploying Content," offers complete information on getting your content from the Visual SourceSafe database to its final home.

Chapter 7, "Version Management," tells you how to keep track of various versions of your files, and how to handle switching between the versions of those files.

Using Visual SourceSafe

CHAPTER 4

Visual SourceSafe Projects

The politics of projects

Learn some basic logic on setting up projects, such as the difference between what should be a project and what should be in a project.

Subverting the existing order

Just because you have a bunch of projects already completed doesn't mean you can't use Visual SourceSafe. Adding existing files is all the easier, since you can judge the scope of a completed project far more accurately.

You've already read quite a lot about projects. Chapter 1, "Visual SourceSafe Concepts," covered the idea of a project and Chapter 3, "Visual SourceSafe Quickstart," gave you the basics of their use. This chapter goes into more depth regarding organizing projects and how to best insert an existing project. ■

Creating New Projects

If you read the Quickstart you already know how to create a new project (if you didn't read Quickstart, it is covered here, as well). However, to say that you're knowledgeable in project lore would be comparable to claiming to be a good parent because you know how children are conceived. Most of the organizational ideas broached in this chapter are simply common sense, yet it seems that common sense is the last thing people think of when embarking on a project. An important segment of managing a project is actually planning it.

Logical Project Divisions

Project planners are tortured at the beginning of any major undertaking. The people above them in the corporate food chain ask difficult questions such as "How much? How big? How long?" These questions are not only extremely personal, they're also very difficult to answer. Visual SourceSafe can't actually give you the means to predict the future, but what it can give you is a good damage control system. An example of planning for the future is illustrated in Figure 4.1.

The Plans of Mice and Men

Before Jose left for his Hawaiian vacation, he had to sketch a brief outline of what the scope of the Fliedermaus Bank of Zurich's project would be. He already knew that there was going to be a core Web project that would represent the Bank in a traditional Web site. Added to that came the limited ATM functionality, which would comprise a programming project. Jose knew that his programmer, Jeff, was very ornery when it came to independence, so he just made a catch-all "code" project to allow Jeff to make his own divisions. He also knew that Marge had already designed some preliminary graphics for the Bank's site, so he only gave her a simple "Web" project, trusting her to organize things as she saw fit. Lastly, he put a catch-all Miscellaneous directory for administrative documents and the reports the Fliedermaus Bank of Zurich was certain to demand.

Jose was late for his plane, so he left it at four project divisions, a main Bank of Zurich Project, a Web Project, a Code Project, and a Miscellaneous Project. He hoped this would be adequate for any growth situations the project might encounter, and serve as a rough outline.

FIG. 4.1
Jose's first draft at
project organization.

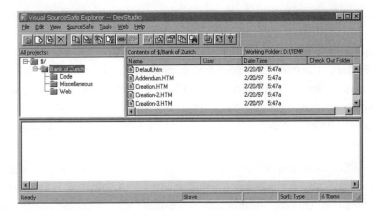

Don't let the size of a project daunt you. One of the great things about the planning process is splitting that huge, mind-boggling project into small, digestible chunks. For large
projects you should adhere to a structure you would use in your hard drive. This does not
mean mimicking your hard drive exactly. As has been mentioned many times before,
there are no organizational constraints on a Visual SourceSafe project's makeup. For small
projects, you shouldn't make things complex. It's a waste of time and resources to put six
files into six projects. The Fliedermaus Bank of Zurich project is composed of a variety of
file types, from graphics, to HTML, to C++ code. Having all of this in one directory would
be an unforgivable mish-mash of disorganization. Project managers have been hung for
less.

Part
II

Ch
4

Creating, Grouping, Embedding Your Project

Before going any further you should probably know how to create a project in the first
place, as well as how to embed one project within another.

1. Choose File, Create Project.
2. Give your project a descriptive name and comment to make it easier to keep
   track of.
3. Click OK.

If you want to create a project within another project, simply select the project you want
filled, and then follow the previous steps.

A good rule of thumb is to group like-file types. The more important issue, though, is embedding projects within each other. Right away you have to determine which project is the most important, or which is the *root project*. The project method of organization is similar to the traditional drive tree because the project listing's "geography" is variable. The problem with this variability is that it's quite easy to give precedence to a project or an aspect of a project that isn't necessarily the most important. You can easily switch a project listing's importance and layout in a project just by dragging its contents to another location.

Site Corporati has decided to organize its projects based on the client name, followed by the applicable projects being done for that client, followed by the requisite file directories, and so on. This approach becomes unwieldy when you have a large client base, or don't often do more than one project per client. The majority of Site Corporati's work is Web design-based, so sorting by job type is not a concern. What if the client base were much larger, and demanded a variety of different tasks? The organizational emphasis changes from tracking clients to tracking jobs. A reorganization of the root project structure based on tasks would become necessary, so instead of Fliedermaus Bank of Zurich, Web, Images it would become Web, Fliedermaus Bank of Zurich, Images. This might seem like quibbling about how to correctly spell "potato," but choosing the right model of organization is a very important thing.

Is your project going to grow? Then make room for it by mapping out projects now so you don't have to do it later, in an expansion-crazy haze. It's always better to follow a plan than it is to make one up on the spot, and hope you'll remember it next time you have to reorganize. A good motto to keep in mind when creating specifications is that it is much easier to delete than it is to create. Following this rule, Jose's original concept of the project outline is laughably simple, but he was in a hurry to catch his plane. Hopefully his subordinates will be able to wrangle things into shape. However, you don't always have that luxury. Only the project coordinator or Visual SourceSafe administrator should have the power to change some projects. If you set up a strange, counter-intuitive project schema, your co-workers are forced to follow it or not use VSS at all. In this sort of situation, the best you can hope for is open communication so you can revamp the project to everyone's satisfaction.

Even if you do misjudge things disastrously and your project explodes like an overshaken beer can, you can reorganize things to fit. New projects are created within each other, and their contents can be moved around with the ease you've come to love in a graphical user interface.

Feeding Your Project

The project is nothing without the files. You can walk around all you like, bragging of "dozens of projects on the go," but when your boss checks them and finds them empty, you're out of a job. Remember, you're not constrained to one project. If a directory is full of files that are all hanging out together, there's no rule that says they have to stay that way when put into a project. The Visual SourceSafe database in no way reflects the status of the original file on the hard drive.

However, all of these theoretical musings do you no good if you don't actually know how to add files to your projects:

1. Choose File, Add Files.
2. Either enter a directory path or browse to the location of your files.

If you have a morass of different files to add, fret not. Visual SourceSafe follows all of the Windows conventions for selecting files. If you want to work from the file list in the Add File dialog box, you can hold down Ctrl and select items one at a time. Holding down Shift and clicking two files will choose every file between those two points. You can also choose from some of SourceSafe's possible file types from a pick list, or enter a wild card extension on your own in the text box. The Add Files dialog box is illustrated in Figure 4.2.

Part

II

Ch

4

FIG. 4.2
With Visual Source-
Safe's selection tools
at your command, you
can narrow a large
field of possible files
in order to single out
the ones you need.

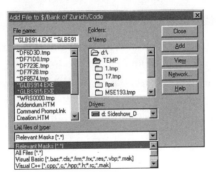

Trouble in Paradise

Jeff the programmer goes to add all of his relevant files to the Visual SourceSafe database. Halfway through, he realizes that Jose's original project of "code" is far too basic and optimistic, so he shuffles and drags things into a more workable shape. On his hard drive, Jeff actually stores his object and library files in the same directory. He realizes that it makes more sense to split them into two different projects. Because the project is being programmed on a function-by-function basis, Jeff also needs somewhere to store his fully tested and ready-for-prime-time code. He drags the applicable files into his new Object, Library, and Completed Projects. You can see the organizational structure in Figure 4.3. To round things out, Jeff sends off a memo to Jose, berating him for not thinking things through more thoroughly.

FIG. 4.3

Even though Jose originally set up the project structure, Jeff has the power to make changes within his own areas.

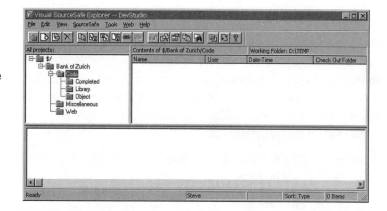

An important factor to consider here is if a file even belongs in a certain project. People often go into a file-adding mania and add anything that isn't nailed down to their Visual SourceSafe project. This is fine, because the only practical limit on a Visual SourceSafe database is hard drive space. However, your employer may not take such a practical view, and start bothering you about things such as efficiency, cost-to-use ratio, and so on. The importance of selective file adding becomes much more apparent when you are integrating an already existing project into the Visual SourceSafe database.

Inserting Existing Content

The odds of your obtaining Visual SourceSafe and having nothing at all to add to it are slim. The reason you get the software in the first place is in part the future return on project development times, but also because you know VSS can protect your existing documents. Fortunately, the question in this case isn't "Can Visual SourceSafe integrate existing documents," but instead, "Which files should I add to the Visual SourceSafe database?"

Adding Old to the New

Marge the designer had already done some graphics in order to demonstrate to the Fliedermaus Bank of Zurich that Site Corporati could fulfill its needs. Now she finds that she can easily incorporate some of those graphics in the real site's design. Bringing up the directory listing on her screen, Marge is dismayed to discover that she has scattered graphic files all over her workstation hard drive. Not only that, but she has also used an obscure file-naming system that she realizes immediately will confuse anyone but her. Using Visual SourceSafe's selection tools, Marge winnows down the scattered files into one "images" project, a branch of the Web Project. In order to avoid confusion she comments each file as it is added, as shown in Figure 4.4.

While she's there, Marge decides to roll up her sleeves and define her own work area. She copies across the traditional Site Corporati Web structure since it's the one she's used to. In addition to Web, Marge has added an Images Project, having the subprojects of Titlebar, Menu, Photo, and Advertising.

FIG. 4.4
Don't be shy about your comments. The more information the better.

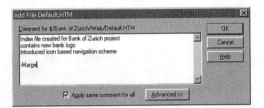

Integrating existing material is like searching for that elusive prize at the bottom of a cereal box. You might end up with the prize, but you've also got a handful of cereal flakes for your troubles. When you consider the size of some projects before they're organized, well, that's several cereal boxes. To make your newly inserted project a lean, mean, and efficient one, you have to ensure that you get only the files you need. Ask yourself these questions to determine the priority of Visual SourceSafing your files:

Part
II

Ch
4

- **If lightning struck your tower unit, would you commit grisly ritual suicide because you no longer had a copy of this file?** These sorts of files are the reasons people invent Revision Control Systems in the first place. Generally, sensitive programming code, original graphics, financial statements, and original project specifications fit into this category. In the case of Site Corporati, Jeff's code, Marge's graphics, and Jose's plans should be stored somewhere outside of their respective workstations (the Visual SourceSafe database, for example). These sorts of files are an "A" priority, and should be processed as soon as possible.

- **If an earthquake opened a chasm underneath your workstation, would your boss be annoyed by the loss of this file?** This is supplementary material that isn't irreplaceable, but might cost you a few days work and the displeasure of your supervisor. Site Corporati's analog would be contact information for the Fliedermaus Bank of Zurich, or Marge's preliminary files. These files are a "B" priority and should end up in the Visual SourceSafe database if you have the resources, but aren't a necessity. Keep in mind that the majority of the computer industry resides on the San Andreas fault.

- **If a clumsy co-worker spilled coffee on your machine, destroying this file, would you bother getting it again?** This refers to the games on your hard drive or executables compiled from your already SourceSafed source code. These files should never be included in the SourceSafe database simply because they're not important to your project.

Refining a Project's Contents

When Marge was adding the graphics, she came across several of her source graphic files that she used in creating the proto-site. Realizing that having them on hand could ease future work, she creates a new project under the Web, Images called Source Graphics. Now if called upon to create several derivatives of the bank's logo for the site's look and feel, she can do so easily. Her changes are reflected in Figure 4.5

FIG. 4.5
Jose's original project plan was short-sighted, but it did allow for real growth.

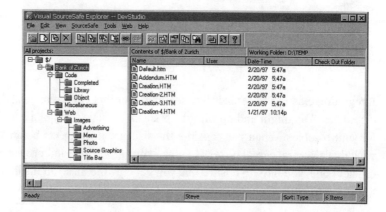

Integrating an existing project is something of a misnomer because it's impossible to actually create a file solely in Visual SourceSafe. The emphasis here, though, should be on integration. It's all too tempting to simply dump in a directory structure lock, stock, and barrel and try to figure out how it works later. Given Visual SourceSafe's extreme flexibility, it's easy enough to simply delete and reorganize a project until it suits your needs—but isn't it nice when you can plan things neatly from the start? Hopefully, one of the reasons you decided to use Visual SourceSafe was the time-saving aspect of having firmer control over the files during the development cycle. You're not saving time if you're monkeying around fixing your project structure. Try to do it right the first time.

From Here...

You've learned that Visual SourceSafe projects aren't like those papier-mâché projects you did in primary school. Not only are they less sticky, but they're also vital to organizing your VSS workspace. While you've learned a lot about creating and manipulating projects, there's still quite a way to go before you can become the coveted Project Master. Study hard, young one.

Chapter 5, "File Basics," tells you all sorts of things you can do to the projects you've just lovingly created, including deleting them.

Chapter 8, "Controlling Projects," lets you in on the secrets of multiple-user files and how to handle changes to them.

Chapter 12, "Visual SourceSafe Administration," is an overflowing cornucopia of information dealing with the ins ands outs of managing a VSS installation.

Part

II

Ch

4

File Basics

Visual SourceSafe mimics your existing file system in so many ways it should be re-released and called VSS 97. The file manipulating power of the Visual SourceSafe system is great, and you should learn all the tricks possible within its repertoire; that way you can impress your friends at parties with disappearing and reappearing file tricks, among other amazing feats. You learn all that and more in this chapter. ■

The lowest common denominator

Learn how checking in and checking out are the basic functions that make up the Visual SourceSafe philosophy.

Random acts of generosity

Everyone should learn to get along and be selfless, kind human beings. Visual SourceSafe encourages this philosophy with its file sharing features.

Cloak and dagger

Protect yourself from damaging side projects by hiding them in plain sight.

Checking In and Checking Out

The two basic commands for manipulating files in the Visual SourceSafe database are check in and check out. Any changes you try to make to any of the files (aside from deleting them) must include these two processes. A check out borrows a file from the VSS database, much like a library book. You make your changes to the file, and then check it back in, returning it so Visual SourceSafe can store your changes. That said, the first thing you should learn to do is check out files from the Visual SourceSafe database, so you can edit them in safety. Before you do that, however, you should understand the check out process and why it always comes first.

The check out process requires three things before Visual SourceSafe will allow it to go through—an actual project and a file to check out from that project. The last thing needed is a working directory that becomes the file's temporary home while working on it.

▶ **See** Chapter 4, "Visual SourceSafe Projects," on **p. 41** for more information on projects.

Storing the Working Directory

Deciding where to store your working directory can have ramifications beyond simply cluttering up a "temp" directory. For example, a check out request comes in, and Visual SourceSafe prepares itself to copy your file into the working directory. However, the defined working directory is the original home of your file. This can mean two things: first, you can make your changes and save the file, overwriting the original file on your hard drive. This is bad because:

- It effectively eliminates the need to check a file back in, or to get it elsewhere, removing two layers of Visual SourceSafe's protection scheme.

- It also means changes get made, and you might forget to check a file back in because, according to your memory, those changes are already set in your original copy. They are not set in the database, however.

On the other hand, overwriting original files can be a good thing: it allows you to update your files almost instantly, having only to deal with checking out a file. The only problem lies in remembering to always check back in from your original directory instead of a temporary, working one. Ultimately, it's your decision, but checking files out in this fashion can turn Visual SourceSafe into a glorified backup dump instead of a true revision control system.

N O T E Sometimes, changes not entering the Visual SourceSafe database can be a good thing. This is almost always the case when you make a disastrous mistake and don't want to preserve it. You also may change files for testing purposes that you don't want inside the database. That's why you have a check in command in the first place. ■

To change your working directory you can press Ctrl+D or mouse over to File, Set Working Folder.

Birth of a Working Directory

Because Jeff is a programmer, he wants to keep files in a fairly hierarchical fashion. He also wants to keep them around for an extended period of time. In accordance with this, his working directory is a large, rambling structure into which he checks out files most of the time. Jeff's projects depend on a large number of files, so he has to have something in his working directory most of the time to aid compilation. He only checks files in after making changes to them, and most of the static files are checked out quasi-permanently. This is but one way to host a working directory.

Marge's design projects aren't as rigorous in their demands. At most, she would need six or seven files at one time. She simply maintains a single, temporary directory that she has Visual SourceSafe purge every time she resubmits a file. The Web development cycle is much shorter than that of a program, so the single directory is all she needs.

Checking Out a File

Defining your working directory is the most complex aspect of checking out a file or project. The actual steps following are quite simple, as shown in Figure 5.1:

1. Highlight either a file or project from its respective listing by clicking it.
2. Select SourceSafe, Check Out.
3. If you haven't defined one yet, you'll be asked to define a working directory.
4. A copy of the file/project will be automatically moved to your working directory.

Within the check out dialog box, the Recursive check box only appears when you are checking out an entire project, as opposed to a file or a set of files. This option applies to any subprojects contained within the project you want checked out, and whether or not Visual SourceSafe should also check them out.

The Don't Get Local Copy check box seen in Figure 5.1 refers to whether or not Visual SourceSafe will overwrite that file if it already exists in the working directory. This is handy when you already have a copy in the working directory, and just want permission from Visual SourceSafe to modify it. You could also use this option when you want to replace a file with an older or different file of the same name. In that case, you would copy the file you want inserted into your working directory. Then you would check out the file of the same name with the Don't Get Local Copy check box unchecked. You could then check the file back in, replacing your original copy.

FIG. 5.1

Checked out documents are outlined in red, with the name of whomever has them checked out in the next field.

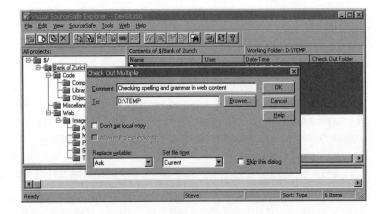

More options are revealed when you open the Advanced tab, shown open in Figure 5.1. The first, Replace Writable, controls how Visual SourceSafe handles checking already-existing files with write permissions enabled into your working folder. Ask will request permission to let Visual SourceSafe overwrite the file. Replace will always overwrite the writable files with the new copy when possible. Skip will disregard the file and generate an error message to the status bar. Merge will attempt to combine the two different files.

▶ **See** Chapter 8, "Controlling Projects," on **p. 107** for more information about project management.

The second pick list, Set File Time, controls what method of date stamping is used to mark the file when it is modified. The Current setting always uses the current time. Modification sets the date stamp at last modification, in case you check out a file but don't actually change it. Check in forces Visual SourceSafe to use the last time the file was checked in. All of these options, including the local file options above, can be set as defaults from the Tools, Options menu. This allows you to set a series of options so you don't have to hit the Advanced tab all the time in order to enter unique settings.

The last check box on the Check Out dialog (refer to Figure 5.1) is called Skip this Dialog, and it tells Visual SourceSafe to use the default values for all of the Advanced options. If you have set no defaults, it uses whatever settings you used last. You can get this dialog box in two different ways after clicking Skip this dialog. The first is by resetting the check box from the Command Dialogs tab in the Tools, Options menu. The second is to hold down the Shift key while checking out a file.

Your check out process can end in one of two ways. The first occurs only in the case of mistakes, and is the Undo Check Out option. You can go to SourceSafe, Undo Check Out to access this function. Generally, you undo a check out for two reasons: you selected the wrong file to check out, or you've damaged the checked out file irreparably, and are better off just starting fresh. The second way to terminate a check out is to check the file back in, completing the cycle.

Check in calls the cows home from the pasture, ensuring they go back in the barn, and get fattened up so you can eat them. In computer parlance, that means you return them to the database so others can access them, perpetuating the development cycle. The checked in files are compared to the Visual SourceSafe database to see if any changes have been made. If there are none, the existing copy of the file is retained in the database, reducing overhead and hard drive waste.

Checking In a File

Checking in a file is just as easy as checking one out, only there are different attendant options, as shown in Figure 5.2:

1. Select a file or project to return to the Visual SourceSafe database.

2. Go to SourceSafe, Check In.

3. Comment your file accordingly and click OK to check the file in.

FIG. 5.2
The Check In dialog box allows you to influence many factors dealing with a file's reception.

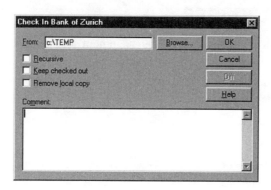

Part
II

Ch
5

The Recursive option found in Figure 5.2 applies only to project level check ins, as files don't have a project structure to recurse. This option determines whether you check in only the project you selected, or all of the subprojects descending from that folder. This option can obviously save you a lot of work when it comes to sprawling project structures with several embedded subprojects.

The Keep Checked Out option determines how Visual SourceSafe treats a file after you've checked it in. If you want to continue working on it, and bypass the trouble of checking it out again, click this check box on. It maintains a file's checked out status after you check it in. This means the file is still available in the working folder. This lets you work with less interruption, and encourages you to check in after every major change to a file.

The last check box option, Remove Local Copy, refers to Visual SourceSafe's disposition toward a file after you check it in. If the box is checked, VSS will delete the copy of the file in the working directory. If it is not, then the file will remain there until you remove it by hand. If you are short on hard drive space, this is an option that will help you conserve space, because it deletes files after you are done with them instead of letting them linger.

The Diff button is short for Differences. Put simply, it allows you access to past incarnations in that file's lifetime.

▶ **See** Chapter 7, "Version Management," on **p. 85** for more information about Differences.

The comment box is a huge, gaping, white space waiting to be filled. Your method and frequency of entering comments is very important to tracking your projects' overall movements. Commenting is a good practice to get into, and even a simple statement of the date and what changes were made is better than nothing when it comes to figuring out just why a file was checked out.

Internal Maintenance

Every database system needs an internal management scheme. If there weren't one you'd have to decompile Visual SourceSafe and pore over obscure code every time you wanted to change something in the database. Luckily, Visual SourceSafe has those kinds of tools, and even luckier, they're easy to use.

Moving Projects

One of the more important commands is the Move Project function, which allows you to move a project from one project to another. You would want to use it when a file's utility for one project has expired, but you want to transfer it to another. An example of using the Move Project command is displayed in Figure 5.3.

N O T E   The Move Project command is handy for shuttling projects around from various departments. If Jeff needs a bunch of files with no strings attached, Marge can put them in a project and move them to the location Jeff prefers. ■

To move a project all you need to do is:

1. Select the project you want to relocate.

2. Go to File, Move Project.

3. Use the Explorer interface to determine where the project ends up.

4. Click OK.

FIG. 5.3
The Move Project command lets you rearrange your project layout to your heart's content.

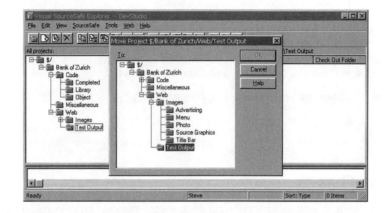

> **CAUTION**
> You might think you're all sneaky and smart if you just bypass the Move Project command, and instead just click 'n drag your project to its new home. Well, you'd be wrong. Dragging a project only shares it. Sharing is covered in more detail further along in this chapter.

There is a caveat attached to the Move command, however. Once you've moved a project, it loses all affiliation with its former parent project, although it maintains its history. You also cannot move a project outside of the current Visual SourceSafe database.

Renaming Files

Renaming files is as easy and basic a process in Visual SourceSafe as it is in your operating system. The repercussions of renaming a file in VSS are surprisingly light, given the software's propensity for tracking things. The file's history remains unchanged, and if the file is shared across several projects, it is concurrently renamed in all of those projects.

Cross-Platform Woes

Marge currently designs on two machines, a Macintosh and a PC. Unfortunately, she was careless when originally adding her HTML files and saved them all as .HTML. Her PC system doesn't want to recognize a file with a four-character extension, instead preferring its own three-character system.

Luckily for Marge, she thought of using Visual SourceSafe's rename function to clear up her problem. She renamed all the files . HTM, and all she has to do to make the name change current on her PC is check out all the files.

The renaming process is exactly the same as it is under Windows 95 convention. However, instead of clicking a file's name twice you:

1. Select the file or project you want to rename.

2. Choose File, Rename.

3. Replace the existing file name with the one you want and press Enter.

Deleting Files

To quote a famous, obscure man, "Files were made to be deleted." This isn't really the Visual SourceSafe philosophy, but it's still a required side of any software package. In VSS you have two ways to handle the sad duty of deletion.

The first is a recoverable delete, which allows you to get the file back if you want. It's removed from any of the projects' file listings, but still exists in the Visual SourceSafe database. The second option is *destroying* a file. After getting destroyed, that file is kaput. Either method is sufficient for removing a file's entry from a project listing. To delete a file or project:

1. Select the file or project from its appropriate listing.

2. Choose File, Delete.

3. If you want to destroy this file (delete it permanently), click the Destroy Permanently check box.

4. Click OK.

5. Click OK again to verify that you want to delete the file.

Whoops! Everyone makes mistakes. As mentioned earlier, if a file isn't destroyed it can be recovered. Visual SourceSafe keeps the file around in the database so it can be reconstructed if need be. If you want to recover a file or project, follow these steps and cast an eyeball over Figure 5.4:

1. Select the project out of which that file was deleted.

2. Call up the Properties of that project by either right-clicking it or going through File, Properties.

3. Switch to the Deleted Items tab.

4. Select the file you want to recover.

5. Click Recover.

FIG. 5.4
The Deleted Items tab lets you recover deleted files or destroy them entirely with the Purge command.

If instead of recovering a file you want to delete it permanently, you should click the Purge button, pictured in Figure 5.4. This removes the file from the VSS database just as effectively as if you had destroyed it in the first place.

Like the vacuum cleaner and the 24-hour maid service, all of these tools are invaluable house-cleaning utilities. However, their importance is eclipsed by the power of sharing files between projects and users—the ultimate team game.

Part
II

Ch
5

Copying and Sharing Files

Visual SourceSafe is great for those hermit programmers who live on mountains, never interacting with others, and glorying in the absolute safety of their files from savage beasts or elements.

Unfortunately for the rest of you with jobs, you actually have to work with other people. Usually you have to work with them on the same types of things. This means you have to overcome your selfish human nature and learn to share. Visual SourceSafe helps you take that first step in the 12-step sharing program by letting you share your files with others.

Visual SourceSafe stores all of its files in an internal database. You already knew that. But one of the factors that makes this database powerful is the ability to eliminate overhead by sharing files between projects. In the old days before nitrogen, they just used to copy the file twice and let each person use his or her copy as each wanted. This was a clumsy hack of a solution.

How Compromise Leads to Peace

Marge and Jeff are not the best of friends, despite being co-workers. They rarely see eye to eye on anything, so any technology that puts another layer of disassociation between them is a good thing. Unfortunately, the nature of their work is such that they actually have to occupy the same building.

The Fliedermaus Bank of Zurich is a demanding, petty client. It is always submitting changes to the project depending on what its current chairman of the board is thinking. However, it pays enough so that the people at Site Corporati ignore their revolving door tendencies.

With the project still in its seminal stages, there are plenty of "hot off the press" changes sent in by the Bank of Zurich's marketing director, Dan. Because both Jeff and Marge need access to these files, and because Jose updates them in the first place, this information is shared across the project. This means that if Marge updates the file, Jose and Jeff's copies immediately reflect those changes.

Sharing the file also means there's markedly fewer staff meetings at Site Corporati, something that all three employees are grateful for.

To say that Visual SourceSafe can copy files is inaccurate. If you want an actual duplicate reflecting the file's state at that time, you would have to add it to two different projects. This quickly becomes a pain, as you are maintaining two copies. You change one, you have to quickly change the other in order to stay current. The Visual SourceSafe database also has two copies of the file floating around in its database when one would easily suffice. That's why you can share files. This process is displayed in Figure 5.5:

1. Select the project with which you want files shared. This is the project lacking in files to which you will be sharing.
2. Choose SourceSafe, Share from the menu bar.
3. In the dialog box that pops up, browse to the project from where the shared files are coming. This tells VSS where to get the files.
4. Select the file or files you want to share using the selection tools in the dialog box.
5. Click the Share button.
6. If you've shared all the files you want, click the Close button. Otherwise, repeat Steps 1–5.

FIG. 5.5
A Shared Document
icon appears as three
small sheets of paper
atop one another in
the file listing, as
opposed to the
"normal" icon of one
sheet of paper.

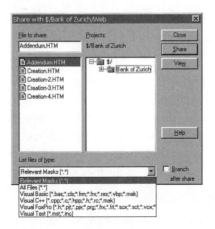

As always, Visual SourceSafe gives you a variety of selection tools to use, ranging from a
file type pick list to entering wild cards. The dialog box also contains a check box labeled
Branch After Share. A *branch* is a portion of a project that has branched off and gone
another route. This is important for sharing because the branch's state can be frozen or
rolled back to a different version. This lets whoever has shared that branch make sure the
file doesn't change when they may still need a particular version of that file. Clicking the
check box creates a branch with the selected files in it immediately after you share them.

▶ **See** Chapter 8, "Controlling Projects," on **p. 107** to learn more about branches.

T I P None of the wily Visual SourceSafe veterans muck around with all that menu stuff. They take the
direct approach, dragging the files into the project to be shared.

Part

II

Ch

5

If you're sharing a project, it's a good idea to first organize the shared files' intended destination, as you cannot set a destination once you have entered the Share dialog box. This is
mostly a good thing, since it makes you plan ahead instead of just cluttering everything
with shared files. Remember, sharing is a healthy experience, and hopefully, if you set a
good example, you can set aright today's skewed values.

Searching for Files

Visual SourceSafe was designed to operate on a large scale. You don't install a revision
control system on your computer just to keep track of baking recipes. No, you do it to
monitor those hordes of data that run over you like the sewer outflow from a New York
estuary. The problem with locating everything in a centralized database is that files accu-
mulate. They conglomerate into this huge gummy mass, and in order for you to find what
you want, you have to go in there with a miner's helmet and a pickaxe.

Searching through thousands of files, one by one, is a slow and tedious process that consumes valuable money-making time. It's fortunate that Visual SourceSafe's designers foresaw this problem and provided the tools to help conquer it.

The primary search engine has two different settings for an incremental search. The first is the familiar wild card search, which allows you to search by file name, extension, or any combination of the two. The scope of a wild card search can be adjusted. It starts at the smallest possible unit—the current project. The next level is the current project and all of that project's subprojects. Finally, you can choose to search all of the projects in that database. To start a wild card search you must do the following, as shown in Figure 5.6:

1. Choose View, Search, Wildcard Search.

2. Enter the wild cards or partial strings you want to find.

3. Choose the scope of your search: current project, subprojects, or all projects.

4. Click OK to launch the search.

FIG. 5.6

To end a search, press Ctrl+Q. This returns the Explorer to normal browsing mode.

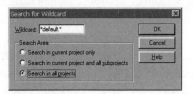

The second variety of search's criterion is a file's status. The status search will only list files that have been checked out. To narrow the search, you can force the search to return files that have been checked out by a certain person. The status search also has the same scope variables as the wild card search, current project, subprojects, or all projects. To launch a status search as illustrated in Figure 5.7 you must:

1. Choose View, Search, Status, Search.

2. Decide whether you want to search for all checked out files, or only those files checked out by a certain person.

3. Select the scope of your search: current project, subprojects, or all projects.

4. Click OK to launch the search.

N O T E Initiating a search process puts the Explorer in *search mode*. This means that your normal file display is filtered to show what results your search turned up. If all of your files suddenly disappear after you do a search, it means you forgot to cancel the search from the File, View menu. You can also press Ctrl+Q. ▪

FIG. 5.7
Use the Status
Search to track down
checked out files on
a person-by-person
basis.

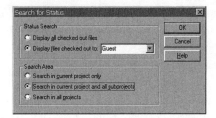

The search is a very effective tool for tracking down a file's name, but what if you want to search for something by a file's contents? The question that has long plagued scientists has finally been solved in this implementation of Visual SourceSafe. The Find in File command is just what the doctor ordered.

Find in File searches a project's files for a string of characters that matches its search criterion. The strength of this search lies in the fact that it looks inside the files, and not at the file name or some sort of keyword or label list. Find in File also lets you screen which files it will look into by using a file name match. To start a Find in File search you must:

1. Select a project or file to search through in the Explorer.

2. Choose Tools, Find In Files.

3. Select in which file (if any) you want the search to occur.

4. Enter the string you want to find.

5. Click OK to bring up the search result box.

FIG. 5.8
Find in File only works
on text files.

Part
II

Ch
5

There are a couple of options available on the Find in Files dialog box (displayed in Figure 5.8) to further help you refine your search. The Item field contains the opening range for the search. If you enter the root project $/, then the search can possibly encapsulate the entire Visual SourceSafe database. The String field is the actual string for which you are searching, and can be augmented by the use of wild cards. In clicking the Match Case check box you force the search to only display results that are capitalized exactly the same way your search terms are. Use Regular Expressions doesn't allow the String field to contain wild cards, and forces Visual SourceSafe to treat them as literal characters. Having the Recursive option checked means the search will also go through every subfolder that may have a link to the Item field. Enabling List all Shared Files Separately makes the search results keep track of how many projects a shared file is linked to. If this option is not checked, the shared file will only show up under its original parent project.

 TIP Although the Find in Files dialog box can handle wild card characters in its search criterion, you might want to insert a *literal* * while still being able to use ? as a wild card in the <u>S</u>tring field. A literal is a character that is normally a wild card, but in this case you want it to actually represent itself. To insert a literal into a string you have to preface it with a backslash \. Following that insertion, * becomes \ *. The previous ? becomes \?, the previous \ becomes \ \. Of course, if the Use Regular <u>E</u>xpressions option is checked, all of these become literals and your search will probably tank.

Even though it's not actually a search type, the sort function can help you organize and find files, especially in environments where there are hundreds, perhaps thousands, of files in a project. Sort can organize the file listing by five categories: Name, Type (extension), User (user who has that file checked out), Date and Time, and Check Out Folder. In order to sort the file list as shown in Figure 5.9 you must:

1. Select the project whose file listing you would like sorted.

2. Choose <u>V</u>iew, S<u>o</u>rt and select by what criterion you would like to sort: Name, Type, User, Date/Time, or Check Out Folder.

FIG. 5.9
Sorting the File Listing can save you time and energy tracking down an elusive file.

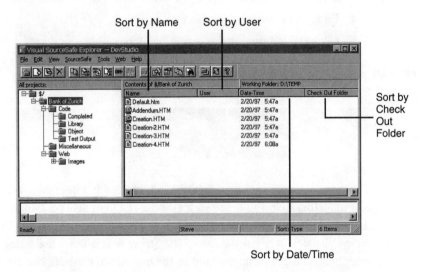

You can also force the Visual SourceSafe Explorer to sort directly by clicking one of the named bars above the File Listing. For example, clicking the Date-Time bar will sort the files in chronological order.

File Properties

Everyone has his or her attributes. Some people are fat, some have blue hair, and others write technical reference manuals. Files are the same way, except they don't actually have hair. Viewing a file's properties lets you see the little foibles that the file hides from all the other guys at the read/write head. You can view a file's properties by either right-clicking the file and choosing Properties from the menu that appears, or you can:

1. Select the file or project whose properties you want to view.

2. Choose File, Properties.

A file's properties are divided into four basic categories; you can navigate through them using the tabs at the top of the dialog box. The first is the General tab.

General Tab

The General tab contains general information about the file, such as its name and project path, its type, the version and date information, and the file comment. An example of the General tab is shown in Figure 5.10

FIG. 5.10
The General tab is the only tab shared between project and file properties.

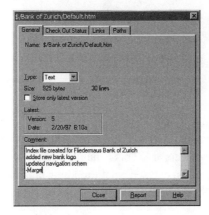

Part
II

Ch
5

You can change the file type from binary to text or vice versa. This is a handy feature because Visual SourceSafe treats both file types differently, and it makes things easier to be able to override some of the program's internal archetypes. You can also click the Store Only Latest Version check box to eliminate Visual SourceSafe's delta method of storage. Instead of storing the original file and the cumulative changes to it, SourceSafe will hold onto only the most recent version. This generally takes up less hard drive space at the expense of losing VSS's version control ability. Lastly, you can change the comment to suit whatever mood you're in when viewing the properties. To view the next tab, click

Check Out Status, which is immediately next to General. The Check Out Status tab is pictured in Figure 5.11.

Check Out Status Property Tab

The Check Out Status tab contains all of the relevant information dealing with the file's current check out session. The details include file name, check out type, username, date/time, version number, computer checked out on, the working directory, and the full project path. All of this data is useful for determining who's doing what to a file, especially if you aren't the one who checked it out in the first place. The only change you can make to the Check Out Status tab is to the comment. To access the next tab, click the Links tab.

FIG. 5.11
The Check Out status property tab tells you all the juicy details about its current check out. If the file's not checked out, it's pretty boring to look at.

Links Tab

The Links tab has a simple purpose in life—to tell the world what projects the file is shared with, and where those projects are. This is handy when you think you know a file is shared, but aren't sure where. You can see what the Links tab looks like if you take a look at Figure 5.12.

You can also see how many other people are sharing a file you've made. To view the last file property, click the Paths tab, as shown in Figure 5.13.

Paths Tab

The Paths tab will tell you two things: the first is whether this file is in a branch, and what that branch's status is. The second is how many versions of the file exist, and more importantly, what version the current file is. In the oft-confusing world of branches and shared projects, this information can be quite handy when trying to determine which versions of a file to use in which branch. Lastly, there is a Links button that duplicates the functionality of the Links tab in a small dialog box.

FIG. 5.12
The Links tab can often clear up the confusion of determining which file is shared by what project.

FIG. 5.13
The Paths tab contains advanced information for keeping track of branches and versions.

Project properties aren't nearly as complex as their file counterparts. There are only two tabs in the project properties, and the first is essentially a mirror of the file properties General tab. The only difference is that instead of being able to choose a file type, you can set whether or not a project is *cloaked*. Cloaking a project protects it from any inadvertent bumbling on your part. You can see a cloaked project, but you can't affect it unless you decloak it. The Deleted Items tab is another story altogether.

Deleted Items Tab

The Deleted Items tab contains a list of all the items ever deleted but not destroyed in a project's history. If there are any items in the deleted list, you have two options in dealing with them. The first is to recover the file and reincorporate it into the project. The second is to callously purge the file, never to be recovered. If you're a little too fast with the clicker finger, you'll probably be spending a lot of time looking at the screen pictured in Figure 5.14.

FIG. 5.14
With a careless push of the Recover or Purge button you control the destiny of countless files.

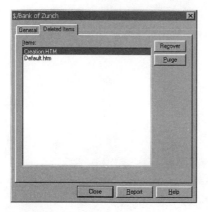

Cloaking Files

Not every project in the Visual SourceSafe database is one you need to see or work on. However, there's always the danger that through a recursive function you'll do some damage to a totally innocent side project. The Cloak function allows you to protect yourself against just such an occurrence by announcing, "I want nothing to do with this project, I wash my hands of it." From then on, you can only access the project implicitly. It will never be included in a recursive function unless you decloak it. This sort of discrimination is handy for projects with a high degree of specialization, so that people with a very tight focus can concentrate on their work and not worry about influencing someone else's.

"What, Me Worry?"

Jeff is not a perfect programmer, although he claims to be a perfectionist. When a mistake is made, he invariably tries to blame someone else. When Jose introduced Visual SourceSafe to the office, Jeff lost most of the excuses in his blame-shifting repertoire. No longer can he try and point the finger at someone else "messing with his projects."

Almost as soon as Visual SourceSafe was installed, Marge cloaked all of the non-Web projects. Jeff may continue to make claims that he is not at fault, but at least Marge will have some safeguards, proving she couldn't have done any damage.

In order to cloak or decloak a project you need to do the following:

1. View the properties of a project, either by right-clicking it or Choosing, File, Properties.

2. In the General tab, click the This Project is Cloaked for Me check box to either cloak or decloak the project, depending upon its original status.

FIG. 5.15
Cloaking: Helping stop public enemy number one—you.

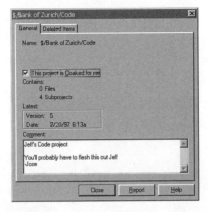

You now know the basics of file manipulation in Visual SourceSafe. However, this chapter is only the introduction to larger concepts, that deal with the World Wide Web and administering your own VSS installation.

From Here...

That's quite a mouthful of information isn't it? Make sure you chew this chapter over, because there's a lot to be learned about Visual SourceSafe's file operations. Keep it up, and you could be the one who everyone in the office turns to for help. To increase your knowledge even further, you should check out:

Chapter 6, "Deploying Content," which covers the specifics of publishing to Web servers and other remote machines using Visual SourceSafe's Web Projects feature.

Chapter 7, "Version Management," tells you how to manage the history of a file, how to commit changes to a file you want saved, and how to exclude the errors that you don't want.

Chapter 8, "Controlling Projects," contains information dealing with files being edited on two different machines and how to integrate conflicting changes.

Part
II

Ch
5

CHAPTER 6

Deploying Content

So, you're ready to go live. Ready for prime time. Your Web site is motivated and ready to show the world what it's made of. Now what? After all of your work and familiarization with the VSS processes, you are ready to deploy your Web site for the perusal of the masses. ■

Going for the gusto with *Get*

Who says you can't have fun deploying on a LAN? Make your work a reality by publishing your site to a server on your LAN. Your co-workers will admire and respect you.

Validating your existence

What's that? You blundered your last Web site's deployment with a bunch of dead links and missing graphics? Fret no more—now you can make sure you have it right the first time by using VSS's link-verifying ability.

And now...the Web!

Web Projects are your friends, and you should treat your friends to the best. Discover the advantages of deploying Web projects, whether you're on a LAN or not. This one's a keeper.

Publishing with *Get*

Having completed your initial development, you're ready to send your fledgling Web site into the world of online testing. Historically, this involved manually copying each of the files associated with your project into the appropriate location for your Web server. If you were on a local area network, you were in luck and did it quickly. If you weren't on a LAN and had to transfer your site over the Internet, you relied on good old FTP—neither quick nor fun. Of course, now you aren't dealing with mere files stored in a directory. How do you copy the contents of your Web site when it only exists deep in the bowels of a database somewhere on your hard disk drive? Enter Visual SourceSafe's Get feature.

Get loosely translates into you telling Visual SourceSafe to get off its butt and copy the most current version of your files to a specific location. By issuing this command, SourceSafe searches deep within itself and locates the file(s) you are Get-ting and copies the contents to a destination directory. You can choose to use either a local directory or a local area network directory by using Windows networking UNC paths. Get-ting does not tamper with your files, nor does it check them out in SourceSafe. It simply takes the last checked in version of your files as a basis for duplication.

The SourceSafe Get feature is usually what you use for deployment to test servers or working directories. Although you can use it to publish to your Web site's final destination if your server is on a LAN, you really should use the newer SourceSafe 5.0 features for Web project public publishing and link verification (more on this later).

Getting Ready for *Get*

Once you have decided to start your deployment, you must decide what exactly you are deploying. One of the niceties of the SourceSafe Get feature is its ability to copy a file, a series of files, or an entire project. This allows you to initially deploy a full Web site and then deploy only the changed files for each of your updates. After you've identified the files you need to Get, you also need to identify your target or destination directory. Your destination directory may be your working folder or it may be your Web server's root directory. So, before you start Get, have your checklist ready:

- Identify what project(s) or file(s) you need to deploy.
- Determine your deployed file's destination(s).
- Have ready any usernames and passwords you may need for network access.

Marge's Adventures with *Get*: Part I

Jose spent the latter part of the week in communication with the Fliedermaus Bank of Zurich. Interested in seeing the progress on its Web presence, FBoZ (as the development team has grown to refer to it) requested Site Corporati post a preview on a secure server. Ever eager to please the people who sign the checks, Jose instructed Marge to post the site on a private Web server for the bank personnel to view.

After consulting with the Information Systems (IS) Manager for the Web server information, Marge compiled her list of files to post to the temporary server, as well as the destination directory. Her notes included:

> *Project to Get*: `$/Bank of Zurich/Web`
>
> *Other Files*: `$/Bank of Zurich/Miscellaneous/Notes.HTM, Timeline.HTM`
>
> *Destination Directory*: `\\WebServer2\InetPub\WWWRoot`

With this information at hand, Marge sat down and got to work.

Behavior from the *Get*-Go

`Get` behavior is predictable. When you are retrieving a file that is not already present in the destination, SourceSafe simply copies the file to the destination. If a file exists in the destination directory, Visual SourceSafe performs a few quick checks and determines if the file is identical. If the file is identical to the one you are retrieving, Visual SourceSafe ignores the `Get` and does not modify the file. If the file is different from the master copy present in SourceSafe's database and the local copy is read-only, Visual SourceSafe replaces the local copy with the one from the VSS database.

In the event that your local copy has not been set to read-only, Visual SourceSafe tries to be helpful by assuming you're currently working on the file and you have checked it out. In this case, it does not replace the file. This is the default behavior for Visual SourceSafe, unless you specifically change it in the Visual SourceSafe Explorer Options.

Part II

Ch 6

> **N O T E** Always remember to check in your work so that the most recent changes are available for a `Get`. If you have completed a series of edits but have not checked in your file, the `Get` will not duplicate your most current edits. Instead, it will copy the last version checked into Visual SourceSafe. A word to the wise: always check in your work after you have completed working on it. ■

Doing the Deed

All right, you have your files or projects selected. You know your destination. You're ready to Get with the best of them. The task of carrying out a Get is actually quite simple. You will find yourself carrying out Get actions without even thinking about the process. Let's walk through the process in its most basic form.

1. Open the Visual SourceSafe Explorer and select the file or project you want to deploy.

2. Using the right menu button (while keeping the same file or project selected), choose Get Latest Version.

N O T E You don't always have to right-click to Get your selection. You have the option of either pressing Ctrl+G or selecting SourceSafe, Get Latest Version from the menu bar. ▪

3. The Get dialog box appears, as shown in Figure 6.1. You may accept the default To path (the working directory for the project), or enter a new directory path in this box. You may choose the Browse button to use the GUI to select a path.

FIG. 6.1

The Get dialog box is a wonder in a tiny package.

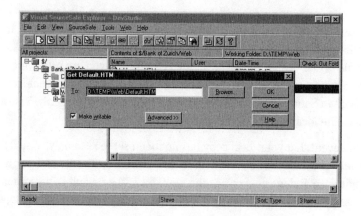

4. If you want your duplicate file to be writable, select the Make Writable check box. By default, Visual SourceSafe copies your files as read-only.

5. If you are Get-ting a project and want to deploy all of the subprojects below it, select the Recursive check box. This will force a new Build Tree check box to appear.

6. If you want to ignore the working directory structure assigned to the project, select the Build Tree check box. A mirror of the project structure will be created in the destination directory.

7. Click the Advanced (>>) button to expand the dialog. Two drop boxes appear: Set File Time and Replace Writable.

8. To define what time and date stamp your file will use, make your choice from the Set File Time drop box. The default is set to the current date and time.

9. If you want to control how your new files write over any files of the same name, select your preference from the Replace Writable drop box.

10. To banish this dialog from your future Gets, click the Skip this Dialog check box.

FIG. 6.2

The Advanced options for the Get dialog box let you determine the GET's behavior before you deploy.

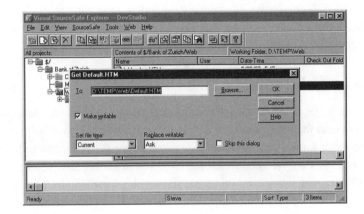

11. Once you are satisfied with the directory path and options, click OK to deploy your files.

If your selected destination directory does not exist, Visual SourceSafe will ask you if it is all right to create the directory. Additionally, you may encounter a confirmation dialog box to replace files, dependent on your Visual SourceSafe configuration and the contents of your destination directory.

You may optionally set Visual SourceSafe to ignore the Get dialog box. To do this, select the Skip this Dialog check box in the Get dialog box. By doing this, you are telling Visual SourceSafe that all Get actions you carry out should go directly to the project's assigned working directory. If you choose this, the default Get behavior is used for all future actions.

Part
II

Ch
6

Marge's Adventures with *Get*: Part II

Sitting down at her desk after lunch, Marge gets down to some serious Get-ting. Pulling her notes up, she quickly launches the SourceSafe Explorer and navigates to the project she needs to deploy ($/Bank of Zurich/Web). She makes sure all of the files inside the project are checked in and up-to-date for the bank people. Content that all is well, she starts the first step by deploying the initial project to the Web server, using the directory path provided to her by the IS department.

Verifying Links

If you have ever dealt with publishing a Web site, you've probably experienced the dreaded *dead link*, or missing graphic, at least one time. You have likely experienced this with your own Web site, due to a typo in your code or an accidental omission in the content deployment. Visual SourceSafe 5.0 introduced a few new features specifically marketed at Web developers like yourself, including the ability to validate hyperlinks within a file. Before exploring this feature, you need a crash primer in Visual SourceSafe Web Projects.

Welcome to Web Projects 101

Web Projects, as introduced to you in Chapter 1, "Visual SourceSafe Concepts," are projects that are flagged as Web content to be delivered to a Web server. Because SourceSafe knows exactly what these projects are, it knows how to handle them. Before you can use the "Web-centric" features of Visual SourceSafe, you must define your project as a Web Project. Once you get past this niggling detail, SourceSafe happily dotes at your side and obeys your Web commands.

Web Projects are simple to create. You need access to the Visual SourceSafe Administrator for your database to set up your project. Ready to create your Web Project? Pull up your monitor; here you go:

1. Within the Visual SourceSafe Explorer, make sure that you have created your project and that you have access to it.

2. Close the VSS Explorer.

3. Launch the VSS Administrator and select Tools, Options.

4. From the dialog tabs along the top of the Options dialog box, choose Web Projects, as shown in Figure 6.3.

5. The top text box, This Project Represents a Web Site, lets you enter the SourceSafe path to the project you want transformed into a Web project. You can click the Browse button to use the graphical user interface to select a project.

6. Enter your Web site's URL into the second box, URL. Your URL should be prefixed by http://.

7. If your Web site uses a subdirectory, enter it in the Virtual Root text box. Do not enter the leading slash (/).

FIG. 6.3
From the Web Projects tab, you can create and modify Web projects from existing projects in your database.

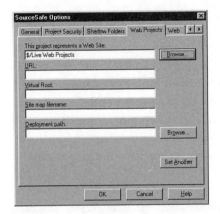

8. The fourth text box, Site Map Filename, lets you specify the site map file name for your Web site. If you do not enter a file name here, Visual SourceSafe defaults to SITEMAP.HTM.

9. Deploying your Web site requires a place to which you can deploy. You enter where you want your Web site to be published in Deployment Path, the bottom text box.

N O T E You can enter deployment paths as a local directory path on your hard disk drive (C:\InetPub\WWWRoot), a Windows networking path for a local area network device (\\Server\InetPub\WWWRoot), or an FTP URL if you are publishing over the Internet. If you are publishing using an FTP URL, you must enter it with the ftp:// prefix. You may specify a username and password for the FTP destination by entering them in the format of: `ftp://username:password@ftp.server-address.dom`. You can specify more than one path by separating with a comma. ■

10. Now that you've set the options to your satisfaction, click the OK button. If you want to set up another Web Project, click the Set Another button to repeat the process before clicking OK.

▶ **See** Chapter 12, "Visual SourceSafe Administration," on **p. 153** for more information about Web Projects

When you reopen the database in Visual SourceSafe Explorer, you can see that the project listing has changed slightly. The icon to the left of your newly transformed project has changed to a small folder with a globe on it, identifying it as a Web Project. In addition to this subtle visual clue, the options from the Web menu are now accessible to you when you work with this project.

Part
II

Ch
6

Doing that Verifying Thing

Now that your project has found its new calling as a Web Project, you're ready to put your pages through the paces. Although not complete on its own as a "do it all, tester of your code," Visual SourceSafe can save your hide on more than one occasion if you're using the hyperlink validation feature. You can choose to check the links of a single file, or an entire project. When you are checking an entire project, Visual SourceSafe processes each file individually and notifies you of any possible problems. Additionally, you can check either the master copy of the files in your SourceSafe database, or your local copy in your working directory if it is present.

N O T E   To use the link verification feature on your working copies, your files must be writable. Make sure that the read-only attribute is not set on the files before carrying out the action. ■

Before you take the plunge into your first link verification, you should brush up on a few points. First, Visual SourceSafe does not validate outside links (that is, links to external sites through an http:// or ftp:// URL) and mailto links (for electronic mail). SourceSafe only checks files within the same project (or working directory) that you reference with relative file paths. Links are checked for the following HTML tags: `<A HREF>` references, `<IMG SRC>`, `<OPTION VALUE>`, and imagemap (.MAP) files. SourceSafe does not check the links to addresses created using client- or server-side code.

Here's how you can check your links:

1. Select the file or project for which you want to check the hyperlinks.

2. Choose Web, Check Hyperlinks. Hyperlinks dialog box, as shown in Figure 6.4.

FIG. 6.4
Use the Check
Hyperlinks dialog
box to validate your
hyperlinks.

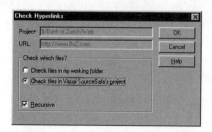

3. Use the radio buttons to choose whether you want to check the files within your project or the local files in your working directory.

4. Select the check box for recursive checking in order to tell Visual SourceSafe to check all files in your project. If you are checking a single file, this option is grayed out.

5. Click OK.

The Check Hyperlinks Results dialog box appears, as shown in Figure 6.5. This dialog box reports to you how your files fared in the link verification. The dialog is broken into three distinct divisions. The first box lists the files that you have checked, the number of invalid links in the file, and the number of ignored links. By selecting a file from the top box, the second box lists the invalid internal (local) links in your file. The bottom box lists the links that were not checked in the selected file. Once you are satisfied with the results, click the OK button to close the dialog box and return to the Visual SourceSafe Explorer.

FIG. 6.5
The Check Hyperlink Results dialog box reports how your files measured up in the verification.

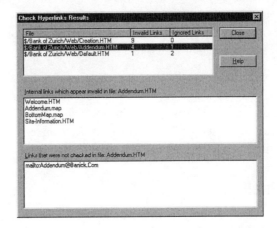

Marge and Link Verification

Pleased with what they had seen in the preview, the FBoZ people instructed Jose to deploy the site to a live Internet-based Web server for release. Jose called upon Marge once again to set the site loose—this time onto the live Web server the IS department had set up specifically for FBoZ's purposes. Jose carefully warned Marge to ensure the site was fully functional and not to let any dead links slip through onto the live site.

Marge, somewhat indignant over Jose's insinuation that her code could cause any dead links, sat down at her workstation and began to verify the links for her project. Much to her own surprise (and chagrin), the SourceSafe link verification reported a series of errors that had slipped by in the latest edits. She quietly fixed the errors and prepared to deploy the site, making sure not to mention the potential recipe for disaster that had almost come to light.

Part
II
Ch
6

Publishing Web Projects

Once your site has passed the initial testing phases and cleared the dreaded link test, you're ready for prime time. The public release of a Web site is a nerve-wracking experience for even the most experienced of developers with nerves of steel. The task of manually deploying all of the files and associated images to the Web server can be a horrendous task. In addition to the basic deployment of the site, the basic administrative issues of compiling a site map and confirming each file's presence can break even the most jaded of Web people.

Visual SourceSafe's Web Projects simplify the process by automating several steps. First, you no longer have to manually copy each file. The SourceSafe Web Deployment feature is essentially a hyped-up Get, tailor-made for Web developers. This new Get is capable of deploying your files to a local directory, a local area network drive, or an Internet accessible FTP site. This isn't your father's revision control system.

Second, Visual SourceSafe handles the tedious tasks of confirming each file and building a site map in one function. On each deployment, you can choose to have SourceSafe build a complete and up-to-date site map, listing each linkable page in your Web site that you have successfully published to the server. You can use this site map for your own reference, or even link it directly into your Web site to ease navigation for visitors.

Getting Ready to Publish

Much like Get, you need a plan for your deployment to your live server. It was one thing to squeak by on your test bed, but now you're going live. It's either do it right and claim the fortunes, or do it wrong and go back to the fry cook line. Before you even consider hitting the OK button on a deployment to a live server, you need to ask yourself a few questions:

- Do I have all of my content ready?
- Is this the right time to publish this content?
- Have I checked in all of my files?
- Are all the links in my files verified?
- Do I have my Web server information ready?

Once you can honestly say yes to each of these questions, you're ready to go for broke and make it live.

Deploying Your Web

Like the link verification feature, the Web deployment feature requires that you have defined your project as a Web Project (as discussed earlier in this chapter). Normal Visual SourceSafe projects do not allow you to deploy. Because you usually use standard projects to store source code, the standard SourceSafe Get facility is suitable. Web Projects are slightly different in nature so they get the royal treatment. All hail Web Projects!

When you are ready to deploy your Web, you must keep in mind that you only deploy the entirety of the site. You cannot deploy single files individually. This task is still (unfortunately) left to the old routine of either a Get (if your server is on a local area network) or manually FTPing the modified file. To deploy your site, follow these instructions.

1. Choose Web, Deploy from the menu bar.
2. If you have want to override your default deployment path, hold down the Shift key when choosing to deploy. The Deploy dialog box appears, as shown in Figure 6.6.

FIG. 6.6

Going against all the odds, specify your deployment path in the Deploy dialog box.

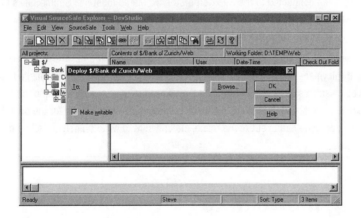

3. In the To text box, enter the deployment path for your Web site. Click the Browse button to use the GUI to select a path.

N O T E How do you enter a name and password in an FTP URL again? Simple to do, this technique also works in your World Wide Web browser. Format your URL like this:

```
ftp://username:password@ftp.server-address.dom
```

Replace username with your account's username, password with your account's password, and ftp.server-address.dom with your appropriate FTP server address. ∎

Part

II

Ch

6

4. You may want to protect your site from accidental changes. Select the Make Writable check box to allow edits to the deployed site. Leave it blank to have the deployed site set to read-only.

5. Click the OK button to deploy your site.

The status frame of the Visual SourceSafe Explorer reports the deployment status, including what file you are currently transferring. You may also encounter dialog boxes asking you to confirm the creation of target directories on your first deployment. If you want to allow all files deployed to directories to be created and files overwritten, you can choose "Yes to All" and bypass having to select "Yes" on all subsequent dialog boxes. Your Web site is now live!

Marge Becomes a Publisher

Having saved face by using the Visual SourceSafe hyperlink verification facilities, Marge is now ready to deploy the Web site for Fliedermaus Bank of Zurich. Because the live Web server for FBoZ is not connected to the Site Corporati LAN, Marge must use SourceSafe's ability to deploy via FTP. Using the username and password provided her by the cranky IS department, Marge sits down at her workstation and gets ready to deploy.

Because she wants to guarantee that it's done right the first time, Marge goes over her checklist for deployment and confirms that each file is ready to go. Once she is satisfied that everything is up to snuff, she quickly deploys the Web site from the SourceSafe Explorer and carefully monitors the status. Everything clears okay, meaning Marge is done for the day! With her work done early, she heads out of the office, making sure to wave politely at Jeff on the way out. He hates that.

Creating a Site Map

Whenever you want to create an up-to-date map of your site's contents, you can choose to do so from the Visual SourceSafe Explorer. This file is a simple, if not plain, page that contains a list of all of your Web "pages" and a hyperlink to them. Because the page has already been marked up in HTML for you, you can easily place the file directly into your Web site for navigational purposes. A screenshot of a sample site map file is shown in Figure 6.7.

Creating a site map for your Web project couldn't be easier than, well, one command. Obviously, the site map feature only works on an entire project, and not a single file (now that would be a remarkably useless site map...). To create a site map for your project, follow these easy instructions:

1. Within the Visual SourceSafe Explorer, select the Web project (indicated by the globe-folder icon).

FIG. 6.7

VSS provides you a simple means of cataloging the pages in your site. It lists pages, and sorts them according to the subdirectory.

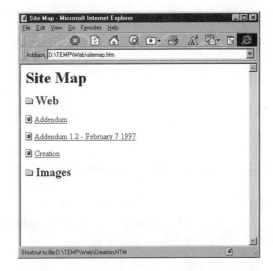

2. Choose <u>W</u>eb, Create <u>S</u>ite. The Create Site Map dialog box appears, as shown in Figure 6.8.

3. Specify a destination directory (local directory or LAN path) in the <u>T</u>o text box. You can use the <u>B</u>rowse button to locate your destination.

FIG. 6.8

The Create Site Map dialog box: the tried and true method of specifying a destination directory.

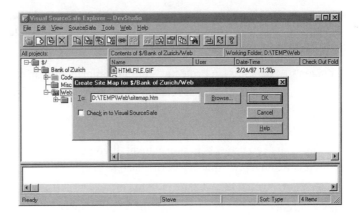

4. Select the Check In to Visual SourceSafe check box to add your newly created site map file to your Web Project. This tells VSS to add the file to your SourceSafe database for all future work.

5. Click the OK button.

Your site map file is now present in the destination directory. To use a site map with the deploy feature of Web projects, create your site map and check it into Visual SourceSafe. This assures you that your site map is delivered with the rest of your Web site upon publication.

Jose's Site Map Debacle

With Marge gone for the day and the Web site up and operational, Jose was truly satisfied. Enjoying a break while reading a book, he was interrupted by a telephone call from Fliedermaus Bank of Zurich. (Collect, of course. It's a bank, after all.) The FBoZ people wanted a complete list of all pages created in the site thus far, for tracking purposes. They also wanted a main map of all pages available from the Web site in case people got lost in the daunting world of banks online.

Jose panicked, not quite sure what to do with Marge out of the office. Flipping through Marge's notes, he came upon her handwritten instructions on creating a site map in Visual SourceSafe. Jose sped to his workstation and launched the Visual SourceSafe Explorer. He hurriedly created the site map file, per Marge's instructions, and e-mailed it to the FBoZ people. Saved again!

Eminently pleased with himself, Jose made a mental note to keep more up-to-date with the project's operations. He then promptly went back to his book.

From Here...

Now that you have successfully published your Web site and verified that its hyperlinks work, you are ready to tackle more pressing issues, which are covered in these chapters:

- Chapter 7, "Version Management," takes you into the wacky world of version tracking. Indispensable for Web developers, these are the tools that make Visual SourceSafe so great.

- Chapter 10, "Backing Up Projects," contains information on shadow folders. Although they're discussed in relation to backups, there is also discussion on automated site deployment.

- Chapter 12, "Visual SourceSafe Administration," explores the issues of administering your Web projects in more detail. If you are looking to maximize your SourceSafe know-how, this is a good place to brush up.

- Appendix B, "Visual SourceSafe Options Summary," provides you a convenient one-spot reference for customizing both the Visual SourceSafe Explorer and the Visual SourceSafe Administrator. Rather than flip around between chapters for information, refer to this convenient resource for information on options.

Version Management

Imagine you had a version control system for your life: deciding you didn't like version 31-years-old, you could roll back to version 18-years-old. That's the level of control you have over a file or project's status using Visual SourceSafe's version control tools. ■

Monitoring files

Reward your good files by including them in your projects. Punish your bad ones by destroying them. Do it all with Visual SourceSafe History services.

"I can't see the difference, can you see the difference?"

Learn what separates working files from bug-ridden ones with the Differences service.

Removing this label can result in federal prosecution

Give your files pet names like Binky or Fuzzins with Visual SourceSafe's labels and keywords.

Version Tracking

You've been told again and again: Visual SourceSafe keeps track of multiple versions of your files, from cradle to grave. But what's that mean? Well, first of all, it means that the size of your files grows each time you perform a check in/check out operation. It also means that you can access your file at any stage in its lifetime.

In the old country, they didn't have this high technology stuff. You had to write everything down. In the past, when people tried to enact history services, they did so by creating a copy of the file for every set date. They would then organize those files in a dated directory structure, resulting in hundreds of files, and an extremely tangled directory tree. Another method is a selective backup, storing the files in an archive on a daily, hourly, or monthly basis. The problem remains in retrieving them in an orderly fashion. The flaw common to these, and indeed all, previous version control systems is that you had to deal with the files on a one-on-one basis every time they were changed. It became a matter of quantity over a really tight organizational scheme.

Visual SourceSafe uses a reverse delta system to store changes. The original file is written to the database when you add it. Every change you then make to the file is stored *relative* to that file. Instead of storing two copies of your file, Visual SourceSafe stores a change to that file. If you were to edit a file and change a "the" to a "that," SourceSafe would simply add a note to its database, "'the' changed to 'that'." This is obviously smaller than storing two copies of the files, yet it can still add up on large projects.

However, the power it grants is exceptional. You can decide to roll back a file's changes all the way to its first incarnation if you so desire. Horrendous mistakes can be corrected quickly and easily saving hours, money, and karma. This feature is a very powerful one, but another problem presents itself: How do you wade your way through all these tiny little iterations of a certain file? With all the changes made between check ins and check outs, it's difficult to ascertain which version is a hugely important modification, and which is where you snuck your name in front of a co-worker's on the credits section. What you need is a way to track Visual SourceSafe tracking your changes.

History

History services allow you to navigate through all those versions and changes, and hopefully allow you to find where you made that fatal typo. The accumulated changes and version information for a file are referred to as its *history*. Visual SourceSafe uses a file's history to help you keep track of the changes you have made. VSS combines a graphical user interface with presenting you all the information you need to pick and choose among versions. In order to get the full interactivity in selecting a file's history for viewing, you need to activate the History Options dialog box:

1. Choose Tools, Options.
2. Select the Command Dialogs tab.
3. Click the History check box under the options relating to files, and not the options relating to projects.
4. Click OK to close the options dialog box.

N O T E It's important to realize that there is a difference between a file's history and a project's history. This chapter deals exclusively with file histories. To learn more about project histories, check out Chapter 9, "Working in Teams." ■

This sets up Visual SourceSafe to always present the additional options dialog box before you engage in any history services. To access the history of the file itself, you have to do the following, as illustrated in Figure 7.1:

1. Select the file whose history you want to view from the File listing.
2. Choose Tools, Show History.

FIG. 7.1
The History Options should really only be activated when you have a large number of versions of a particular file.

You can restrict which versions will appear in the history dialog with the History Options dialog box. The From field refers to the first version number at which you want to look. The To field is the upper limit on how many versions you want to appear. Both of these entry fields should only contain a numeric version number *unless* you have clicked the Labels Only check box. In that case the From and To fields refer to a string found in one of your labels (labels are explored in more detail in the next section), and not the version number. Filling out the User field restricts the search to versions that were created by only that user. If you check Skip this Dialog, the dialog box will never appear again until you reactivate it, using the previously outlined steps.

Part
II

Ch
7

N O T E   You have to be careful of cavalierly activating and deactivating Option boxes for command dialogs. While you can amuse yourself for hours turning the interactivity on and off, there are consequences. Whenever you click the Skip this Dialog check box, it tells Visual SourceSafe to never show you that particular dialog box until you decide to reactivate it. However, it also saves whatever settings were in that box and uses them as the defaults whenever carrying out that process. This applies to any dialog box that has the Skip this Dialog option. ■

The dialog box referred to in Figure 7.2 is the primary means of navigating through version information in Visual SourceSafe. The large text box is the repository of the most information. From here you can immediately ascertain how many versions of a certain file exist, what user made the changes to each version, the date and time the changes were made, and what Visual SourceSafe action spawned those changes. The row of buttons down the right side control the many processes to which you can subject a file's version.

FIG. 7.2

Daunted by all those buttons? Don't be. By the end of this chapter you'll know them better than your children.

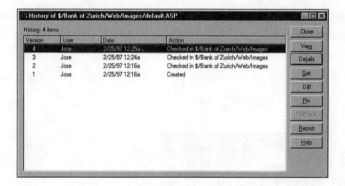

The View button summons whatever viewer you have defined for that kind of file. To define a viewer choose Tools, Options. If you don't have a viewer defined, Visual SourceSafe uses whatever Windows association that file's type may have.

Clicking the Details button will bring up a dialog box presenting more information on the specific version you have selected. It is illustrated in Figure 7.3.

The Details dialog box tells you much of the same information you could see from the History text box. However, in Details you can view and edit the comments and labels attached to a certain version. This lets you keep a running history of your own in the comments field, such as "Rolled back to version 3 on 08/07/74." For more information on labels, refer to the section entitled "Using Keywords and Labels for Tracking," later in this chapter.

FIG. 7.3
The Details option allows you to scrutinize your versions even more closely. It's a history management electron microscope of sorts.

If you throw your eyes over to Figure 7.2 again, you see that Get is the next feature accessible from the History dialog box. Clicking this lets you publish a copy of that particular version to a local location, just as with Get in the Visual SourceSafe Explorer. In this case, though, you are accessing the Get command from the History dialog box, which means you can then publish any of the previous versions of the file with the same process you would apply to the current version. Using Get in this fashion in no way affects the current database copy of the file. There are several uses for this function; most of them progress report-related.

Fun with History

Site Corporati is a pretty laid back corporation. If you got the job done, you can generally keep the hours you want. Jose suspects Jeff of slackery and general malingering, since he claims to "come in and work all night." However, Jeff's work is so arcane, Jose can't really judge very accurately whether Jeff has really done work or just created a bunch of object files. Jose checks a few of Jeff's files' histories and discovers that almost all of the check in times occur late at night, exactly when Jeff claimed to be working. In an inspired fit of managerial relations, Jose decides not to mention his suspicions to Jeff.

File Differences

All of the services in the History dialog box deal with making changes to versions of a file, and its organization is built around that. But what if you needed to know what was actually in the file right then and there? Or, more importantly, if you needed to know what aspect of the file was different from a previous version? What you need to view these details is the Differences function.

Part
II

Ch
7

As its name implies, Differences tells you what varies between one file and another. If you have a working version of a file, and it suddenly stops, you can view the differences to determine what has changed from one version to the next. There are many ways you could do this without using Visual SourceSafe, but almost all of them involve getting the working copy and the buggy copies of the files and printing them out. Then you pore over each file by hand, looking for mistakes. Using Differences is far easier and more convenient. In terms of troubleshooting this is invaluable; instead of going over the file as a whole, you only have to concentrate on the areas that have obviously changed. It's also quite handy when tracking progress.

As in the previous History coverage, you can get more out of your differences if you activate the dialog box that contains more options. To activate the Differences Options dialog box you must:

1. Choose Tools, Options.
2. Select the Command Dialogs tab.
3. Click the Show Differences check box under the options relating to files, and not the options that control projects.
4. Click OK to close the dialog box.

The Differences options allow a great deal more flexibility in comparing files. In the case of a normal, unmodified difference, the most recent copy of the file is compared to whatever copy is in the working directory. However, you are given a whole new level of control when you decide to Show Differences with the additional options enabled. This is shown in Figure 7.4.

FIG. 7.4

Using the Difference options can turn the differences function from a one-trick pony to an entire traveling menagerie. However, if you're only doing simple comparisons, it's a case of overkill.

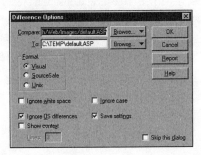

From here you can decide which files to compare. You can even display the differences between two totally different files if you like. The Compare field is the original file that you wanted examined. The To field contains whatever you want to compare that file to. Visual SourceSafe's implementation of the browse function makes it easy to compare files both inside and outside of the VSS database. You can browse files stored in either your operating system or in VSS. From here you can also decide what format you want the differences operation to take. The default of Visual is the traditional side-by-side format you become familiar with later. The SourceSafe mode displays all of the same information but in a single screen format with a breakdown of what line(s) differ(s) and how. There's no bookmark-setting ability, nor is there a search utility. The Unix setting is almost identical, except it uses the nomenclature set forth in the original UNIX comparison program (Diff.), instead of a listing of lines changed, added, or deleted.

Checking the Ignore White Space check box tells the comparison routine to ignore white spaces when calculating differences. This trims out a lot of "overhead" change listings that result from tabs or space bar errors. Selecting Ignore Case allows lines with the same syntax yet different capitalization to be considered identical. This is handy when dealing with cross-platform issues between case-sensitive and non-case-sensitive platforms. The Report button generates a report of the differences to one of three possible destinations: the printer, a file, or the clipboard. There's also a handy Preview button that enables you to see if any differences are generated at all, and whether you should be wasting your time reporting them.

Under the advanced heading is another whole kettle of fish. The first check box is Ignore OS Differences, which tells the comparison engine to ignore the variances in characters between platforms. Mac-, UNIX-, and Windows-based platforms all use different line break characters to denote a carriage return. While these characters fulfill the same purpose, they are not identical across platforms. This discretion is vital for trimming out false changes on things such as different line break codes. When the Show Context Flag is set, the resulting differences will display x number of lines above and below the variance to give you a frame of reference as to why that line might be different. The number of lines to display is set in the Lines box. Clicking Save Settings will save whatever options you have selected for the next time you bring up the Differences Options dialog. The Skip this Dialog check box deactivates the dialog box, and you never see it again until you reactivate it, using the previously outlined steps.

You can get access to file differences in one of two ways. The first method compares the current version in the database against whatever version you currently have checked out. If you have yet to make any changes to the checked out file, the two files will be identical. However, after you've done some preliminary editing and before you've checked a file back in, you can use the differences function to see what changes you have made, and how they compare to the original. This allows you to take a more disciplined approach to making changes, as viewing the differences dialog works as a sort of checklist: "I've made this change, but not that one." To use the first method of viewing differences such as that illustrated in Figure 7.5 you must:

Part
II

Ch
7

1. Check out the file in which you want to view the differences.

2. Make your editing changes and save them in your working directory.

3. Make sure your checked out file is the one selected in the Explorer.

4. Choose Tools, Show Differences in the Visual SourceSafe Explorer.

FIG. 7.5

Differences are usually brought up before checking a file back in. That way you can see what changes have been made and comment your check in accordingly.

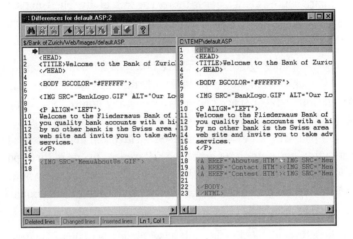

N O T E If Visual SourceSafe tells you that the files were identical although you weren't expecting them to be, there are a few explanations. The first is that you checked the file back in before selecting Differences. Visual SourceSafe compares the current database version versus whatever version is checked out, so if you check your file back in, the two are identical. The second is that you never checked the file out in the first place. Without a check out copy to compare, Visual SourceSafe uses the current database version against your last published copy. If there isn't a file copy in the working directory, you will get an error message instead of a comparison.

The second method of viewing a file's differences is through the good old history dialog box. This method is a different one not only because of the way it's accessed, but also because of how you can make it work for you. The previously mentioned method of viewing differences would compare the checked out copy versus the most recent database copy. When you access differences through the History function, you can choose which version of the file will be compared to the check out version. The differences obtained through History compare the version you select versus the copy of the file in the working directory (not the current database version). Note that there must be a copy of the file in the working directory in order for a differences call to work. You can create one through either checking a file out to the directory, or using Get (Ctrl+G) to publish to it. To use the version selective method of obtaining differences:

1. Select the file you want to examine.

2. Choose Tools, Show History.

3. In the History dialog box, select to which version you want to compare the current (working directory) copy.

4. Click the Diff button.

N O T E   Differences works best on text and text-based files, as it can then display the changes between the files for your view. You can compare binary files, but Visual SourceSafe will only tell you whether the file has changed or not. ■

The Differences function is so powerful because it shows you each file side by side, with what has changed between them highlighted. If there are lines that have been deleted in one file, they are marked in blue in the other. If there are lines that have been changed in one file, they are highlighted red in the other. Finally, if lines have been added to one file, they are marked in green in the other. You can set these colors to whatever you desire from Tools, Options in the menu bar.

In the Differences window, pictured in Figure 7.6, there are several icons running along the top of the window. The first three are used to control the Find command. The first set of stylized binoculars allows you to set basic search criterion and start a search.

FIG. 7.6
Stalking the wily version change with the Find function.

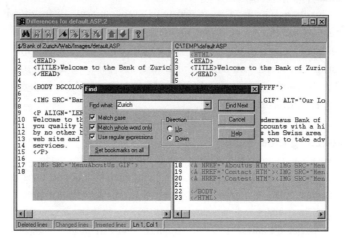

Part
II

Ch
7

As you can see in Figure 7.6, you can set several variables to affect the scope and depth of your search. You ought to be familiar with the first three, as they feature largely in the Visual SourceSafe Search/Find in File functions. Selecting Match Case forces the search to find only results that are capitalized the same as your initial search string. The Match Whole Word Only returns results that are entire words, instead of parts of other words.

For example if you search for "the," it would not return "there," "they," "their," and so on. The Use Regular Expressions option will treat your search string as a literal string. If this option is checked and you try to use a wild-card search such as * or ?, the search will look for actual instances of those characters, without treating them as wild cards. Unchecking this option will allow wild-card searches.

The search *direction* is which way the search engine parses the file. If you choose the Up radio button, the search will commence on all the lines above the currently selected one, until it reaches the top of the file. If you choose the Down radio button, the search continues downward from the selected line, until it reaches the bottom. The Set Bookmarks on All option will take every instance that matches your search criteria and bookmark it. A bookmark is a breakpoint in the file; you can navigate using bookmarks directly instead of paging laboriously down lines of text. The two icons following the Search button allow you to page up and down through items that match your search criterion.

The Search function isn't the only way to set bookmarks. The Flag icon, next to the search tools, allows you to place a bookmark on whatever line the cursor currently resides. When it comes to large projects, bookmarks can be an invaluable tool, especially in cases where changes are relatively few spread over a large area. The icons following the toggle bookmark button allow you to page down, up, and clear all bookmarks respectively.

And finally, the paging tools. They navigate between differences in the two files on a change-by-change basis. The up arrow will move up one difference in the file, and the down arrow will move one down. Once again in the case of large files, paging through the differences can be a valuable aide to navigation. Instead of sullying your hands on the egalitarian keyboard, you can use an autocratic pointing device to navigate through your files. Lastly, on the extreme right is the Help button, which instantly brings up help dealing with the differences window.

Reconciling Differences

Jeff is nearly at the point of tearing his hair in frustration. He has made a minor modification in a file, and the new file refuses to compile properly. No matter how he traces it over he can't determine the cause. In desperation, he turns to Visual SourceSafe's differences utility. He compares the two files and immediately sees the error in the split screen viewing mode. The original line had a comment that was terminated properly; his new addition did not. Jeff corrects the error, cursing the fact that he didn't think of trying a comparison three hours ago.

You notice while scrolling through the two files that the scroll bars are linked. That is, you can't scroll through one without moving the other. This is an optimization to perpetuate simultaneous viewing. It also means that you don't have to constantly adjust two different scroll bars to get your lines to line up. Unfortunately, though, it limits the differences window as a flexible viewing tool. To exit the differences window you must click the Close button provided by the operating system. There is no internal means for leaving the window.

Pinning and Rolling Back

Let's go back to the History dialog box for a moment and learn about pinning and rolling back. Sound like your high school wrestling requirement? Well, you won't find any grunting adolescents in lycra here.

The emphasis so far in Visual SourceSafe has always been the future or the present. "The most current version," or "The newest version." With pin and rollback you're going to learn that latest isn't always bestest.

When you want to pin a file, it means that you want to freeze its development at a particular version. This means that even if new versions become available, the copy the database will use and check out to you is whatever version you pinned. It might seem like backward thinking to deliberately incorporate an older file, but there are quite a few uses for pinning a file. First of all, you may be making such comprehensive updates to a file that you want a "baseline" version always available, so you pin the file to that version. All of your future changes are still stored in the database, and can be accessed through the History functions, but whatever version is pinned is considered the "current" one. Pinning a file is a common occurrence in shared projects. You are making changes to a file that you know other people depend on, so you can't make so large a revision that it doesn't work anymore. You pin the version at a mutually agreeable point, and go on to make your DaVinci-esque changes to the file. In order to stab a pin into a defenseless file you must (as shown in Figure 7.7):

1. Select the file whose version you want to freeze.
2. Choose Tools, Show History.
3. Fill out the History Options (if applicable).
4. Select which version of the file you want to pin.
5. Click the Pin button to freeze that version.
6. If you want to free a version, click the Unpin button.
7. When finished, click Close.

Part

II

Ch

7

FIG. 7.7

You can only pin files, not projects.

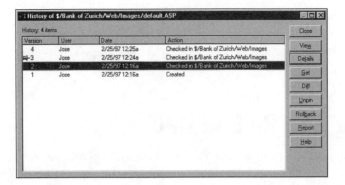

Even though it's important that you be familiar with the pin procedure, it's even more important that you be familiar with the unpin process. The Pin button in the History dialog box changes to the Unpin button when you have pinned a file. When you want to release the pin's constraints over the file, simply select the pinned version and click Unpin.

With the relatively benign pin command comes the equally useful, yet more destructive rollback command. Rollback tells the Visual SourceSafe database to destroy all versions past the copy you specify, and then make that copy the current one. It can be likened to driving a steamroller over a very long snake. The snake is your chain of versions; by driving over part of it you've destroyed the latest versions, and are forced to use the most recent of what's left as the current copy. However, there's still good eating on the rest of that snake, just as whatever version to which you've rolled back is usable, or else you wouldn't have rolled back to it in the first place.

The Search and Replace Misadventure

Marge has been experimenting with new HTML authoring programs, and recently tried one out that has an extensive search and replace function. Marge test drives it and finds it to her taste, and vows to have Jose buy it for the project.

However, unbeknownst to Marge the search and replace actually operated on all of the files in her directory, instead of just one. The changes are radical, yet go unnoticed because it's the end of the day. The next day and two check ins/check outs later, she discovers her error. She quickly goes into the Visual SourceSafe History function and finds the version just before her search and replace mistake. Just as quickly she does a rollback on those files to eliminate the horrendous mess the search and replace operation had created. Marge wonders if she can claim she spent the two workdays trying to learn the new HTML editor...

Rollback is a dangerous operation, and you should only use it when totally certain that you need to. The process is an irreversible, unrecoverable one, and should never be started under the influence of prescription drugs of any kind. That said, here's how you destroy precious files in a rollback maneuver, as displayed in Figure 7.8:

1. Select the file you want to roll back.

2. Choose Tools, Show History.

3. Select the version to which you want to roll back. This will become the current version of the file.

4. Click the Rollback button.

5. Click Yes to verify your desire to destroy the affected versions.

FIG. 7.8
Visual SourceSafe likes to double-check these things, just in case of temporary mental illness.

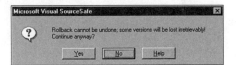

You cannot roll back a project, only files. Aside from delete, this is the most dangerous Visual SourceSafe command you can use. Always plan its use carefully, and don't go around rolling back things half-cocked.

Reports

Generating a report can serve more of a purpose than placating those no-good busybodies in accounting. In Visual SourceSafe, "report" is actually a sort of catch-all term that refers to any output generated by VSS. You can generate several varieties of reports based on what data you want, what service you want, or what menu you are currently using.

Common to all reports is the Files Report dialog box. From here you can choose what form the report will take, be it a printout, saved to a file, or written to the clipboard. You can also preview the report's contents. The dialog box is shown in Figure 7.9.

The most common variety of report is a File list. This report lists the contents of a Visual SourceSafe project, or indeed, all of the files in your Visual SourceSafe database. In order to generate a file list you must do the following:

1. Select the project on which you want to report. Select the root project ($/) to get the entire VSS database.

Part
II
Ch
7

2. Choose Tools, Files Report.

3. Select which output stream to use (file, printer, clipboard) and click OK.

FIG. 7.9
The Report Options dialog box is universal to all reports, and can be used to redirect the data for any report.

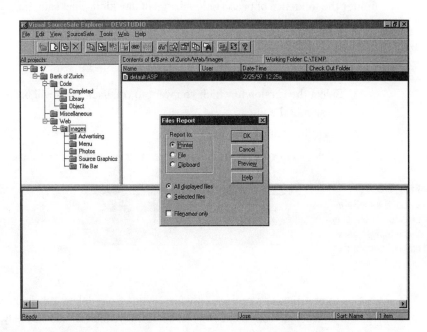

The File listing dialog box has some options to refine the output of the report. If you want a listing of all of the subprojects under the current one, make sure the Recursive check box is checked. If the Include Files option is checked, the report will list all of the files within a certain project. If it is not, then the report will consist of only project names. The Filenames Only option tells Visual SourceSafe to present only the file names, and to trim off extraneous path information. As always, you can get a preview of the output by pressing the Preview button.

Reporting Progress

The people at Site Corporati generate a file listing every day. Both Jeff and Marge's projects have been fully outlined at their point of inception. Because Jose then has a rough idea of what the finished project's file structure will look at, he can compare the existing file listing to the idealized one for project completion. This is a primitive method, however, and Jose doesn't realize that he'll learn a better one in Chapter 9, "Working in Teams."

The only other class of report that has special interactivity is a History report. You can create a History report by doing the following:

1. Select a file or project on which to report.
2. Choose Tools, Show History.
3. Complete the History Options (if enabled from the Tools, Options dialog box).
4. Click the Reports button.
5. Select the output stream (file, printer, or clipboard) and click OK.

The only difference here from other report dialogs are two check boxes that determine what content goes into the report. The first, Include Details, will add the file's details to the report. This includes the date and time, the user who created that version, the check in location, the comment, and the label comment, if any. The second option, Include Differences, will append a report of how the file differs from the current version in the VSS database. If neither option is selected, a bare-bones report of the file's name, version, date, and time is generated.

There are several other means of generating reports; however, they are nothing more than text dumps containing straightforward information. You only need to know File list and History report specifics because of their unique display options. Areas you can generate reports for include: File listing, Find in Files, History, Differences, Links, Paths, and General Properties reports. While you can't generate reports on search results directly, you can create a report of a file listing. Because a search modifies the file listing in the Explorer to represent its results, a file report made before you quit the search would be just as accurate.

Using Keywords and Labels for Tracking

This entire chapter deals with sifting through the Visual SourceSafe database contents and manipulating that information. You learned the file selection tools Search and Sort in Chapter 6, "Deploying Content." You've learned how to differentiate between versions in this chapter. But what if all of this just isn't enough? What if, instead of having to search for something alphabetically and chronologically, you could just give it a unique label that would make it easy to find? Well, "what if" no more. Visual SourceSafe supports this capacity with its implementation of labels.

This isn't your jar of pickles label, either. It's a unique identity tag that you put on a project or file to make it easier to find. Labels also serve a purpose for large organizations. Departments can label certain files as "theirs," and can then know which files were supposed to be used when presented with a choice between similar projects.

Part

II

Ch

7

Before you can understand labeling, it's important to understand versions. In Visual SourceSafe a version of a file is a point in time during that file's existence. If a file's lifetime was plotted on a line graph, versions would be the points. Visual SourceSafe uses an internal version tracking system, based on whole numbers. You generally start at version 1, and for each successive check in and check out that involves a change, the number increments by one. For example, the third time you checked a file in, it would become version 3.

N O T E While it is possible to label a file, it's more a waste of time than anything else. You would have to apply a new label for every check in and check out. It makes far more sense to label an entire project, or to label a file that will remain at that version for quite some time. (A pinned file, for example.)

Visual SourceSafe's internal system is fine for keeping track of things generally, but rarely does a developer want to increment versions in whole numbers. They want to stick things like "2.0b" on a project, or "Alpha Test Mark VI." That's where labels come into play. A label is essentially a user-assigned version number. Visual SourceSafe still tracks its files internally by way of its own versioning system, but if you label something, you've got a little tag sticking off it saying "this was important enough to specifically be assigned a version number." However, it's more than just a label on an existing version. By labeling a project you create a new version of that project, although your project isn't duplicated. Like Visual SourceSafe's internal numbering system, a label isn't maintained. It is only pertinent to that version, and when a change is entered into the system, the label stays on the older version. Using labels instead of VSS's normal versioning also requires a certain discipline, because an infrequent labeling system might as well not be a system at all.

However, there are advantages to labels. For groundbreaking events in your project's development they make a better marker than the impersonal "version 20." They can also indicate states of a project such as code freeze, beta testing, or final revision. As a final tool for keeping track of the labels themselves, you can comment every label entry you make. To actually place a label on a file or project you must do the following:

1. Select the file or project you want to label.
2. Choose File, Label.
3. Label and comment the label as desired.

A label comment is not the same as a file comment. The label comment applies only to that label, the file still has its own label intact. If you label a file or project in this fashion, the label will apply to the current version. If you want to label a past version of a file or project:

1. Select the file or project to be labeled.

2. Choose Tools, Show History.

3. In the history dialog select the version you want labeled.

4. Click the Details button.

5. Enter your label in the appropriate field.

6. Click Close and Yes to save your changes.

Regardless of how you labeled a project, there's only one way to remove a label: Duplicate the previous process, but instead of entering a label, delete the existing one. You have to verify that you want to save the changes again. A file or project that has been labeled is marked with a small tag in the History dialog box, to allow for easier identification.

Keywords work like labels, they are a unique text string that can communicate information and identify a file. However, a keyword is inserted *inside* a file instead of identifying it externally. A keyword is a special Visual SourceSafe reserved word that expands into a variable when it is checked in or added to the VSS database. For example, the keyword $Date: $ will insert the date and time of the file's last check in. Keywords should be inserted into commented code so they don't interfere with your file's contents. Table 7.1 contains all of the Visual SourceSafe defined keywords.

Table 7.1 Visual SourceSafe Reserved Keywords

Keyword	Definition
$Archive: $	Visual SourceSafe archive file path.
$Author: $	User who last changed the file.
$Date: $	Date and time of last check in.
$Header: $	The Logfile, Revision, Date, and Author keywords combined.
$History: $	The File history in Visual SourceSafe format.
$Log: $	The File history in UNIX Revision Control System (RCS) format.
$Logfile: $	Visual SourceSafe archive file path.
$Modtime: $	Date and time of last modification.
$Revision: $	Visual SourceSafe version number.
$Workfile: $	The file's name.
$NoKeywords: $	No keyword expansion for all keywords that follow (colon optional).
$JustDate: $	The date without an hours/minutes stamp.

Part

II

Ch

7

The syntax is simple. The information is inserted after the colon, but before the dollar sign. Using the $Revision: $ keyword would produce $Revision: 87$ within code that had been through Visual SourceSafe's keyword expansion process. If there isn't enough space between the colon and the terminal dollar sign, the output is truncated to fit. This is fine for commenting programming code, but it leaves a lot to be desired for HTML purposes. That's why Visual SourceSafe has special keywords for use in HTML files. These keywords trim out the dollar signs and the keyword itself, leaving only the expanded data. The only difference in declaring an HTML keyword and a Visual SourceSafe keyword is an additional dollar sign preceding the keyword.

You could use keywords more practically in an HTML file, since you can display the data without having the keyword itself attached. The line `<!--$$Revision:--!><!--$--!>` would produce the output of 87 only, because the data would be inserted into the space between the comment tags. (Actually, it would just produce 8 because there's only one space between the comments) Keywords are an excellent combination with HTML because they allow you to have constantly updated information without having to update that information yourself. A Web site could easily have a `date last modified` or `revision #:` line on it that the Web author would never have to edit beyond the first time of adding the keyword.

Easing Harried Minds

Marge is a commenting fanatic. She tries to accurately comment everything she does. Normally this is a desirable trait, but she's finding as the project grows, so do her commenting duties, until they almost match her normal workload. For her, keywords are a godsend.

Marge can now simply add keywords to her files, where before she would always have to update the revision and date information herself. She saves herself a lot of work, and is gloating over the fact that she hasn't told Jeff about this technique yet, when she knows he comments just as much, if not more, than her.

The problem with keywords is that they're pretty processor-intensive. You have to set conditions, and even some options, for their use in making things go faster. Visual SourceSafe defaults with keyword expansion disabled. You have to enable keywords on a file-type by file-type basis. For example, it would be wasteful to scan binaries for keywords. In order to change that you have to do some fooling around in the Visual SourceSafe Administrator:

1. In the Administrator, choose Tools, Options.
2. The Expand Keywords in Files of Type text box is what you want, and it is found on the General option tab.

3. In the text box enter an asterisk in front of each file extension that you'll be using keywords with (*.HTM, *.C, and so on, as shown in Figure 7.10).

4. Click OK.

FIG. 7.10
If you don't enable keywords in the Visual SourceSafe Administrator, VSS won't know what to do with them.

When you check in or add a keyword-bearing file, Visual SourceSafe expands the keyword into the requisite data within that file. You already knew that. What you didn't know is that VSS also performs a `Get` command, placing the latest version of the now-expanded file into your working directory. Some people don't need or even want this sort of service because it drains time and computer resources during check ins. In order to turn this option off you must:

1. Choose Tools, Options.

2. Select the Local Files tab.

3. Click off the Copy Keyword-Expanded Files into Working Folder option.

4. Click OK to close the Options dialog.

Keywords in and of themselves are quite powerful, especially for light maintenance duties, which in the past normally drove coders mad. They also make commenting the body of your files much easier, because you don't have to type in all that information every time you make a change. If you combine labels, keywords, and comments, you have an identification system for SourceSafe files that works both internally and externally.

You've come a long way, baby. This chapter raised you from the neophyte of Visual SourceSafe that you were, to an acolyte, or even a monk, learned in all of its revision control secrets. Reserve a special place in your memory for the options of the History dialog, because it's there that most of your disasters can be rectified. If not, well, there's always the rollback.

Part
II

Ch
7

From Here...

Move onto the next logical levels with

Chapter 8, "Controlling Projects," which gives you the goods on using project branches and shares to help manage multiple teams working on one file.

Chapter 9, "Working in Teams," is the rough equivalent of this chapter, except all of the commands take place on the project level.

Managing Projects with Visual SourceSafe

Controlling Projects

You've mastered quite a few concepts when it comes to dealing with projects, and hopefully by now you realize that they're one of Visual SourceSafe's primary strengths. Organization based along project guidelines is a boon to working practically and efficiently. However, there's an entire subset to using projects that you may not be aware of, which involves the sharing and merging of files. ■

Tree surgery made easy

Experiment with Darwin's theories of convergent evolution using Project branches to diverge your files.

Extend an olive branch

Work in peace and harmony with your co-workers as you share similar files to meet different goals.

Joining of like thoughts

With its project and branch merging functions, Visual SourceSafe is the melting pot of the software world.

Project Branches

You can do a lot with a project. As you've already learned, you can put files in it, share it, destroy it—all the things you could do with Silly Putty and more. You're about to learn another facet of project management—branching.

When you share a project, it creates a share link from one project to the other. There is only one copy of the file between the two projects, and when a change is entered into the original file, that change propagates to all shared files. This is incredibly handy for inserting bug fixes after a project is mostly finished. The key phrase there, though, is "mostly finished."

If you are developing a project in tandem with someone else, and that someone else is constantly changing his or her shared files, it could be confusing. Imagine going back to the shared file and finding it different every time. In code-sensitive situations this is a strict no-no. You could freeze the file's progress using the Pin command, but this would stop the original developer from being able to make revisions as well.

There's another facet to consider: what if the two projects have the same basic structure, but actually two very different results? What you need is some method of sharing the file and then somehow splitting it on a divergent track from its original parent. In Visual SourceSafe terms, this is called *branching*. The metaphor is that of a tree. The original project content is the trunk, and the divergent files are its branches. The branch travels away from the trunk, but is still a part of it. Visual SourceSafe's branches operate in much the same fashion, except unlike a tree branch, they can be reattached to the trunk. There are two ways of creating a branch; both have the same requirements and the same effect. In order for a branch to exist, it must be based on a shared file or project, as shown in Figure 8.1. The first method of branching is available directly from the Share dialog box. To share files so they branch immediately you must:

1. Select the project to which you want files shared. This is the project lacking in files to which you want to add files.

2. Choose SourceSafe, Share.

3. In the dialog that pops up, navigate to the project from where the shared files are coming.

4. Select the file or files you want to share using the selection tools in the dialog box.

5. Ensure that the Branch After Share check box is checked.

6. Click the Share button.

7. Click Close to escape the clutches of the Share menu.

FIG. 8.1

It is impossible to create a branch without first having a shared file.

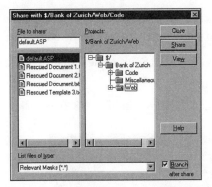

The <u>B</u>ranch After Share option is incredibly important to the process. Without it you have just created another share. With it enabled, however, you have created a share that can exist on two planes. Once a file is branched, it has two copies of itself. Imagine your original shared file as a Siamese twin, joined at the hip. What changes one will affect the other, and both will remember the events that occur. Suddenly, through a surgical miracle, the two are separated, free to live lives of their own. Their paths suddenly diverge, but nothing can erase what has already passed between them. The files operate in a similar fashion. The history of each file is the same until the branch is applied, and then varies depending upon what happens to each file afterward.

Alternate Streams of Development

Jeff is in charge of developing the ATM functionality behind the Fliedermaus Bank of Zurich's Web site. Because he is constantly refining his work and his code, Visual SourceSafe is very useful to him. However, he's reached a point in the project where he has to create the procedures for all of the financial transactions that will take place on the site. He has already built a basic set of routines for the calculations that will take place behind the scenes, except that for every transaction he will have to modify that code a little one way or the other. It would be wasteful to simply include several copies of the basic files when he has access to the power of Visual SourceSafe.

Jeff decides to share the file in each of the transaction sequences projects. He quickly discovers this isn't the correct method, for when he updates code in one of the files, that change is propagated to all of his others. He decides to branch the code files. Each branch is the same original file, but has a separate life. Jeff can now modify each transaction's routines without worrying about changing the other files, and without having to incorporate a new set of files for each transaction.

The other method of branching files also requires you to have a shared file, but in this case you can branch the file long after it has been shared. This would apply to instances when a file is shared, but one of the developers needs access to his or her own working copy. A branch is then put into place. To create a branch you must:

1. Select a shared file from the Visual SourceSafe Explorer. It must be shared.

2. Choose SourceSafe, Branch.

3. Fill out the comment space (as shown in Figure 8.2) and click OK.

FIG. 8.2
Branches should always be commented so you know why you had to put that file on a divergent development track.

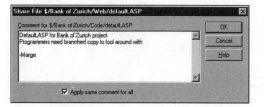

Working with Branches

Branching a project isn't all sweetness and light. Creating a branch from a share eliminates the share link between those two files. This is good when you want convergent development using the same base files, but it's not good when you have to change those base files.

Son of Alternate Streams of Development

Jeff has a slight problem. It turns out that his original financial transaction code had a slight bug. Unfortunately, the ATM transaction project has gotten quite large, and while Jeff has kept everything in its proper project, the sheer volume involved is daunting.

Jeff knows that if the files were shared as they were originally, he would only have to fix one copy of the code, and the rest would propagate out normally. However, since he branched the files, there is no longer a share link between them. This means he has to change the base code files one by one. Unfortunately, because there are so many files, Jeff can't find the ones he needs. To the naked eye, branched files appear as any other. Jeff isn't about to go through his code file by file, but isn't sure what to do...

Fortunately for Jeff there's the paths property. As previously mentioned, branched files are out of the shared propagation loop. In order to implement changes, you have to insert them manually, as you would any other Visual SourceSafe file. The problem is keeping track of all your branched files, and ensuring that they are updated properly. If you are relying on shared files for the majority of your cross-project swapping, it's easy to overlook a branched file. Fortunately, there's a utility to keep track of branchings in the Paths file property.

The Paths file property is a list of all of the current iterations of a certain file. It's particularly useful for tracking down what branches you've generated from a certain file, and where those branches are. To access the Paths property you must:

1. Select the file whose properties you want to view.

2. Choose File, Properties.

3. Click the Paths tab, which is shown in Figure 8.3.

FIG. 8.3

Investigate the alternate existences of your files inside the Paths property tab.

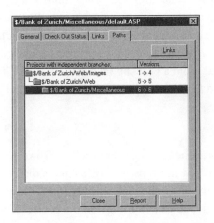

Inside the Paths property window you find the specifics of that particular file's branch history. In Figure 8.3, there are three branches. In the left side of the display area is each branch's actual project location; on the right is the version information for each branch. The version information is presented in this format: *(First version in that branch)* *-> (Current version in that branch)*. The first branch is described as 1 -> 4, which means that it has moved from versions 1 to 5. The second branch, 5 -> 5, means that branch began its existence at version 5 of the first branch but has yet to be modified. The first branch and the second branch share history from versions 1 through 4. The first number in the branch description is at what version that branch was created. In the case of the original branch, the number is usually 1. The second branch was created at version 5, so that's what its starting number is. The second number indicates the most current version. The first file hasn't been changed since the second branch was created, so its most current version is 4. The second branch hasn't been changed at all, so its current version is the same as its original version, 5. If you were to make changes to the original branch and check it back in, incrementing its version number to 5, this would not be the same version as the second branch's 5. Once the files are branched, their histories diverge for good.

All of this heady theorizing about versions might do the eggheads down at MIT some good, but what's the use for Joe/Jane Average? The most obvious is aiding the development of similar projects from an identical code base. Co-workers can share files without having to share a file. Branches can be made quickly and easily, and allow someone else to use your files with no danger of them actually changing your files. You can emulate most of branching's functions that you've seen just by adding another copy of the original file, or pinning a file and then adding that version. Both of these are an additional step that you don't have to execute when using branches. Simply adding another copy of the file does not allow you access to its shared history (like a branched file does).

The concept of branching may be difficult to understand immediately because most of the interesting things related to its use go on in the background. When a file is branched, it is then treated like any other file. It doesn't even have the Share icon attached to it anymore. Branching effectively revokes a file's shared status, bringing it back down to the level of a normal file. What is not normal about a branched file is the fact that its history reflects its shared past, and that branched files can eventually be reunited with their long-lost kin.

Merging Branches

Yes Virginia, you can merge branches in Visual SourceSafe. To continue the Siamese twin metaphor, you would be able to sew the separated twins into a discrete unit once more. Each twin would bring the things he or she had experienced while apart to the union. It's the same with files, although you cannot merge on the project level.

> **N O T E**   You can also merge differing file versions generated by multiple authors. The process is nearly identical, but for more information on multiple user check outs go to Chapter 9, "Working in Teams." ■

When Visual SourceSafe goes to merge two files, it first does its own differences check. After finding out what has changed in each file, VSS compares those changes to one another. If the change in file A has not occurred in file B, Visual SourceSafe creates file C, which would contain the change from file A superimposed over the contents of file B. The resulting file C is an amalgamation of the contents of files A and B. This is an incredibly powerful function, but is also the logical progression of Visual SourceSafe's differences utilities.

You need two different branches of a file in order to merge a file. This means you have to have enacted a branch procedure upon it at least once. To merge branches you must:

1. Select the file you want to merge.
2. Choose SourceSafe, Merge branches.
3. In the Merge dialog box, select which branch you want to merge with your selection (as shown in Figure 8.4).

4. Click Merge.

5. Comment your Merge and press OK.

FIG. 8.4

Merging is one of the more powerful options available in Visual SourceSafe; It allows you to combine the work of two people without actually editing the files.

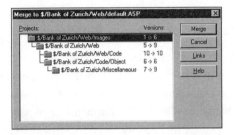

If the versions of the files you merged had no conflicts, then your merge operation ought to have gone perfectly. A conflict is when a line in the merge file and a line in the to-be-merged file disagree. Visual SourceSafe doesn't know how to reconcile those differences, and has to rely on you, the user, to clear them up. If conflicts are not resolved, the merged file is stored in your working directory on a check out. When you want to deal with the conflicts, you try to check it in again. A merged version of a file is not entered into the Visual SourceSafe database until it is successfully checked in. If you can't remove the conflicts or simply want to revert to your original, SourceSafe stores it in the working directory with an .ORG extension. If there is a sudden, inexplicable system lockup or power loss, the temporary merge file is stored in the working directory as well, under the .MRG extension.

Visual Reconciliation   You may have to check in a file more than once, depending on how rigorously you weed out conflicts. There are two methods of reconciling differences in Visual SourceSafe: Visual and Manual. In terms of user-friendliness, the Visual method is superior by far. You can click and drag differences between files, all within the graphical Explorer interface. The Manual merge is a more counterintuitive method, as it doesn't let you make changes on-the-fly. Instead, the Manual merge marks the differences found between the files, which you then have to clean up with third-party editing software. You can set which method Visual SourceSafe uses in the following fashion:

1. Choose Tools, Options.

2. Click the General tab.

3. On the Use Visual Merge pick list, select the Only if There are Conflicts option.

4. Click OK to exit the options dialog box.

There are three settings in the General Options tab that influence which merging method you will use. The first is Yes, which means Visual SourceSafe will always use the Visual merge method. The second setting is No, which means Visual SourceSafe will always use the Manual merge. The third and last setting is Only if There Are Conflicts, which is the happy medium. There's no point in calling up either method unless there are conflicts to resolve. The Visual merge is the most effective means of resolving merge conflicts, and comes heavily recommended. The Manual merge should only be used in cases where you are using batch files or offline processing to eliminate interactivity.

The Visual merge method is more visually complex, but is also more powerful when it comes to deciding what goes into the final merge. The most important element of understanding the Visual merge is mastering its interface. If you checked the Only if There Are Conflicts option, then you won't usually see the Visual merge interface. However, if there are conflicting line changes in your file, you will see the Visual merge editing screen shown in Figure 8.5.

FIG. 8.5

Merging does not work on binary files.

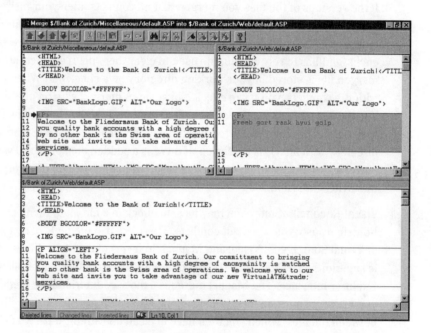

There is no menu bar in the Visual merge dialog; you are forced to rely solely on icons and buttons. They are found at the top of the dialog box, where the traditional menu bar is located. The difference navigation arrows start from the left. Clicking the up or down arrows will move you one *difference* ahead or behind in the file. A difference is a point where a change is present in one file, but not the other. Following those are the conflict navigation arrows. Like the difference arrows, the conflict arrows will move you up or down by one *conflict* through the file. A conflict is a line of text where both files have a different entry, and Visual SourceSafe can't decide which one to use.

The Stylized Binocular icon represents the powerful internal search engine. The first icon allows you to define a search. The next two buttons allow you to skip up or down to the next or previous search item. Next come the bookmark tools. A *bookmark* is a line in the code that you've marked for navigation purposes. You can move up or down through bookmarks much like you can through differences and conflicts, using the same sort of system. The last Bookmark icon will clear all of the bookmarks you've set, resulting in a fresh, clean start.

▶ **See** Chapter 7, "Version Management," on **p. 85** for more information about searching and bookmarks.

The file in the left pane is the one to which you are merging; the one in the right is the file from which you are merging. It doesn't really matter which is which, because the eventual result ends up in the bottom pane, regardless. From the merge dialog you can choose which alteration from which window will end up in the eventual result file. The changes are highlighted and color-coded to tell you what variety of change it is. Deleted lines are blue text, changed lines use red text, and added lines use green text. Areas that have been influenced by a difference between the two files appear outlined in red in the bottom pane. Changes that you have made there from the left pane are outlined in green, those from the right, in blue. Any changed text in the bottom pane appears bold and italicized within its colored outline. You can set all of these colors separately in the Tools, Options dialog.

In the merge screen, the mouse is your friend. What would normally be a laborious job of typing, cutting, and pasting becomes simple point and click. If you left-click any of the conflicts/differences in the left or right panes, they become incorporated into the merge file in the bottom pane. If you right-click any of the conflicts/differences in the left or right panes, you are presented with a small menu. You can choose to Apply that change to the merge file, Remove that change from the merge file, or in the case of a conflict, Apply both changes. When right-clicking an alteration in the bottom pane you can decide to apply the applicable change from the left window, the right window, or both. If you inadvertently go too far changing things, don't worry. There's an undo/redo list as long as your arm. When you're finished you have to close the window in typical Windows fashion—by clicking the x in the upper-right corner.

Closing the window isn't the entire battle. You'll be asked to confirm saving any changes, even if you didn't make any. Click Yes to save, click No to discard all of your changes, or click Cancel to return to the merge window. You have to verify changes regardless of whether you made any because Visual SourceSafe takes care of all the *uncontested changes* before you start editing. An uncontested change is basically a difference, a variation in one file and not the other. By default, Visual SourceSafe adds the missing line to the final merge file. Because of this, you should always be careful when merging.

After you finish reconciling changes, you should be able to check in your file (or it should already be checked in for you). When the merged file gets checked in, it becomes gospel. Until it does, though, Visual SourceSafe uses your pre-merge copy. Trying to check in a file with unresolved conflicts can spawn a dialog asking whether you've fixed all the conflicts. If you have, simply click Yes and the file will be checked in using whatever settings you used while VSS merged it (if any). If you want another crack at merging the file, click No. The file will remain checked out until you've cleared up all the conflicts, or at least claim to have cleared them up.

Manual Reconciliation   With all of its high-powered graphical toys and advanced interactivity, the Visual merge method is quite alluring—but it's not everyone's piece of cake. Visual SourceSafe supports another method of dealing with merge conflicts, which is distinctly nonvisual. With the Manual mode of merging you don't have to do any mucking around in the Visual merge screen. What you must do, however, is use your own editor to make the merge changes yourself. While this method allows a lot of control, it's also much slower and a few steps out of the Visual SourceSafe "loop." When you merge using the Manual method, Visual SourceSafe hunts for conflicts as it always does; instead of prompting you to edit them, it inserts a series of six equal signs (=) to signal a conflict. When going through the file you search out the equal signs and make your own changes based on the context. The Visual SourceSafe = tag is preceded by six left-angle brackets (<). The text after the left-angle brackets is the line from the *master* version, or the equivalent of the left pane in the Visual merge. The actual text following is what the original line appears as in that file. Following the equal signs are six right-angle brackets (>), which contain the text applicable to that conflict from the *local* version, or the right pane. When you merge the files, the resultant file would have the master version's line inside the left-angle brackets, followed by the six equal signs representing the conflict, which is then followed by the line from the local version, ended by six right-angle brackets.

You might want to use the old SourceSafe Manual method of merging if you were merging a large number of files, and wanted to do so in batch mode in order to quickly get them through. The Visual merge is superior in almost every way, but cannot handle more than one conflicting file at a time without human intervention. The Manual merge is for more experienced users who have a lot of merging to do and don't mind using their text editor to do it. The disadvantage of either merge is that your files are checked out until you merge them successfully. This is why you have to check in merged files after completing them instead of having Visual SourceSafe do it for you.

Many of the functions you've learned about in this chapter are very powerful ones for overseeing projects rather than working within them. The shift in perceptions reflects a greater understanding of the power of Visual SourceSafe. Hopefully, you will soon use VSS to manage your file content instead of using it to simply check out those files.

From Here...

Well, you should now know more about merging than any other classically trained scholar. You should be concentrating on managing all those users whose files you've just learned to merge. Hopefully these chapters can help you:

Chapter 9, "Working in Teams," teaches you how to define multiple users so you can edit your own files from several different user accounts, so you can appear busier than you really are (strictly for those suffering from identity crises).

Chapter 12, "Visual SourceSafe Administration," is a quick primer on all the dos and don'ts of ruling your VSS domain with an iron fist.

Working in Teams

Ultimately, Visual SourceSafe was meant for more than one person. You know that you're infallible; you would never damage your own files. That guy down the hall, though, he's so incompetent he couldn't find his own mouse with a cat. You wouldn't trust him with cleaning your office, let alone those nuggets of brilliance that separate you from the accountants. All of the concepts you've learned thus far have been related on a single-user basis, but they're also extensible to team level use. ∎

More is better

Even though they'll invariably do something wrong, you have to give your co-workers access to your work sometime.

Those who do not study the past are doomed to repeat it

You thought History services existed just so other people could catch you when you messed up. Now learn how to catch other people by using a project's history.

Are you allowed to be here?

Make your projects into an impenetrable Fortress of Solitude by using Visual SourceSafe security.

The Multiple-User Conga

Having multiple users in Visual SourceSafe is kind of like dancing in a conga line. You can do it by yourself, but it's more fun with other people. The same dangers exist, too—you need a very powerful leader to take control of a huge conga line, or else people will kick their legs out at the wrong time, stuff will get knocked over, and it's a generally negative experience for everyone. Just like the leader of a conga line, Visual SourceSafe coordinates multiple users, making sure everyone is safe and has a good time.

Multiple Check Outs

Allowing multiple check outs in VSS means that more than one user can check out a file at the same time. This means that parallel development can take place without having to share, branch, pin, or even have two copies of a file in the database. There are many projects in which more than one person has to work on the disparate elements of a single file, which would be impossible (or at the very least inconvenient) without a revision control system such as Visual SourceSafe.

Visual SourceSafe's default configuration is set to disallow multiple check outs. This is because the process consumes more processor time and may lead to confusion when checking a file back in. If you're not sure if you need to have multiple check out access, then you probably don't. The function is reserved for teams that require more than one person working on one file. If you want to have multiple check out access, you have to define that option in the Visual SourceSafe administrator, as illustrated in Figure 9.1.

1. In the Visual SourceSafe Administrator go to Tools, Options.

2. In the General tab click the Allow Multiple Checkouts check box.

3. Click OK to close the dialog box and save your changes.

FIG. 9.1
Make sure you actually need multiple check out functionality before enabling it.

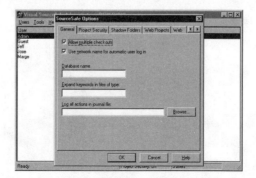

You can just as easily disable multiple check outs by reversing the previous process. Note that the option is *multiple check outs* and not *multiple user check outs*. Visual SourceSafe tracks the processes first by the file, and then by the user. If your company had only one Visual SourceSafe "guest" account for its database, multiple check outs would work just as well as if every workstation had a unique account. The user account can check out the file however often it wants, because it's the file's permissions that have been changed, and not the user's.

While it's important to know how to use multiple check outs, it's even more important to know about multiple check ins, since they control how the Visual SourceSafe database will store your changes.

Checking Files Back In

The really interesting stuff happens when you check the file back in after more than one version of it has been checked out. User A checks a file out. While User A is working on it, User B checks out the same file to make some changes of his or her own. User B checks the file in without incident, because User B was the first to check that particular file in. It doesn't matter who was the first to check the file out; rather, it's who checks it back in first that counts. The Visual SourceSafe database now stores User B's version of the file as its *master* version. User A finally finishes working on the file and checks it back in. How does VSS know which version to keep? The answer is that it doesn't know, so it merges the two files into one, complete whole.

Visual SourceSafe performs a merge operation identical to the merge in Chapter 8, "Controlling Projects." The only difference is in what causes the merge to occur. In Chapter 8 the merge was called because of project branching. Here, it occurs because there are two different versions of the same file that have to be compressed into the same version. When Visual SourceSafe does a merge, it compares the two file versions and determines what changes exist between them. If the two users didn't change the same line when they were editing the file, then the versions are merged transparently to the user. What is the same between both files remains the same, and what is different is integrated into the result of the two files merging. The important factor is that you shouldn't have two edits that have changed the same thing. This creates a conflict in Visual SourceSafe's merging algorithm, which you then have to resolve.

Resolving merge conflicts is not the end of the world, but you should avoid it when possible. You can avoid confusion with clearly defined roles when it comes to who works on what module. The best way to stop merge conflicts is to prevent people from editing the wrong files in the first place. Access should be controlled rigorously. If you check out a file that has already been checked out by its original author, or the team leader, you should try to check in your version first. That way, the more knowledgeable party can control how the merge will occur, deciding which lines remain and which do not. Generally, the roles should be broken down into the well-informed editors and the not-so-well-informed editors. The well-informed should be the last to check the file in, so they can handle the merge properly, catching any mistakes the not-so-well-informed may have made.

▶ To learn more about resolving merge conflicts and the difference between a Visual merge and a Manual merge, please **see** Chapter 8, "Controlling Projects," on **p. 107**.

Project Histories

You already know all about the history of a file, but now it's time to learn about the history of a project. They're eerily alike, yet strangely different. A project's history reflects the changes that have been made to all of the files within that project, during that project's lifetime. This is the ultimate tracker for saboteurs in your company. It also helps discover who's to blame when something goes wrong. To view a project's history you must:

1. Select the project whose history you want to view from the left side project listing.
2. Choose Tools, Show History.
3. Decide which viewing options you desire from the History Options dialog box.
4. Click OK.

FIG. 9.2
The project history display differs very little from the file history display.

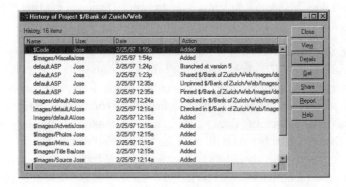

A project's history listing is going to be much longer than your average file's history. That's why the History Options dialog box pops up before you view a project's actual history. A project history is sorted by actions associated with a file as opposed to version numbers. Instead of a listing starting at the first version and ending at the current version, you get information on all of the project's transactions, sorted chronologically. If the project has any degree of age or work associated with it, the list of changes will be quite long. Fortunately, you can filter which changes you want to appear within the project's history from the History Options dialog box referred to in Figure 9.3.

FIG. 9.3
The History Options dialog box allows you to trim the fat on the project's history listing.

History Options

You should be careful when filtering your history listing, as you may remove some of the very results you wanted to see. Selecting your options cannily may mean the difference between a perfect listing and absolutely nothing.

The first option in the History Options dialog box displayed previously is Include File Check Ins. If you don't have this option selected, the history will not include check in transactions in its listing. Secondly comes the Recursive check box. Selecting this will include the histories of every subproject beneath your original project. The third check box is the Labels Only option, which will only list events that have labels associated with them. Even though project histories aren't sorted by version number, you can choose to limit the files displayed by their version. This is what the From and To text boxes are for. The first contains the number of the first version you'd like displayed, the second contains the last.

If you want to view transactions performed by only a certain person, you plug that user's name into the User text area. The resulting history display will contain only changes made by that user while he or she was logged in. The last check box, Skip this Dialog, sets your current options as default and ensures you don't see the History Options dialog box again. You can make any dialog box disappear or reappear from the Tools, Options menu, in the Command Dialogs tab.

Now that your history listing is all nice and configured, it's time to actually look at the project history display itself.

Project History Display

The actual project history displayed in Figure 9.2 is nearly identical to the file history display covered in Chapter 7, "Version Management." All of the relevant information is still in the main text window, sorted by date and time instead of version number. What's missing from the project history window is the View, Differences, Pin, and Rollback buttons. What is present in the project history display but not the file history is the Share button.

▶ For information on creating a shared project or file, **see** Chapter 5, "File Basics," on page **p. 51**.

Tracking the Wily Wumpus

Jose has brought in a few underling programmers to help Jeff program some of the applications for the Fliedermaus Bank of Zurich ATM project. He notices that Jeff suddenly has a lot of free time. Suspecting Jeff of using the underlings to avoid work, Jose decides to look at the history of the Code project and all of its subprojects. Jeff's name appears four times, all over a week ago. All of the most recent entries appear under Underling #1, Underling #2, and Underling #3. Jose uses the report function to generate a hard copy of his evidence and confronts Jeff.

Jeff is indignant but resigned, and gets off with a reprimand. Jose is pleased at the efficiency of Visual SourceSafe in tracking malingerers.

While you can use the various aspects of a project's history to keep track of progress, you can't actually compare a project to an external source. With project differences, you can compare the contents of the working folder with the contents of the project itself.

Accessing Project Differences

History is not the only Visual SourceSafe function that projects share with files. You can also access the differences of a project, much like you could those of a file. The comparison, however, is not identical. Visual SourceSafe doesn't keep track of versions of projects the same way it does files. However, the project is an efficient and contained means of organizing a series of file differences. When VSS does a differences comparison on an entire project it compares that project to the contents of the working folder. You would use this to see what larger changes someone may have made to a project's contents. It also provides a secondary method of finding a file's differences, as opposed to going through the file's history. If you want to track down the differences in a project, you must:

1. Select the project to examine from the Project Listing on the left side.
2. Choose Tools, Show Differences.
3. Fill out the Project Difference dialog box to display the differences you want to see.
4. Click OK.

Much like history, the project differences window can contain a diverse amount of information because it reflects all of the changes made to all of the files in a project. If a project has any seniority at all, it will be chock full of changes, more than you would want to browse through normally. Once again, though, there is a dialog box to help you with your woes. Enter the Project Difference options dialog box in Figure 9.4.

FIG. 9.4

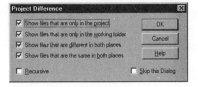

FIG. 9.4
The Project Difference options dialog box allows you to exclude certain transactions and file types from your eventual listing of differences.

Narrowing Your Focus Even Further with File Options

The file options with which you can cull the herd in the Project Difference options dialog box are actually a little different than those found in history. The only two that are carried over are the Recursive and Skip this Dialog check boxes, explained previously in the project history section. The first check box, Show Files that are Only in the Project, trims out files in the working folder that haven't been added to the project you are examining. The second, Show Files that are Only in the Working Folder, displays all the files that exist only in the working folder and not in the project you are viewing. The third, Show Files that Are Different in Both Places, tells Visual SourceSafe to list all of the files that exist in both the working folder and the VSS project, that have differences between them. The last check box, Show Files that Are the Same in Both Places, displays files that exist in both the working folder and current project that have no differences between them.

All of these options allow you to investigate different changes made to the project. If you only want to see files that have been changed recently but are already in the project, you would have the Show Files that are Different in Both Places option checked. If you wanted to see what files have been added to the project, but not yet integrated into the Visual SourceSafe database, you would check the Show Files that Are Only in the Working Folder option.

However, even if you set all of your options perfectly, you may end up with no differences to mine through. This is a crushing blow, and is usually only cured by therapy.

What to Do When No Differences Are Found

You have to remember that project differences have quite a few distinctions from the old and familiar file differences. The first and most important is the fact that the differences comparison compares the current version versus whatever is lurking in the working folder. If there's nothing there, or just the most recent checked out version is present, then you get a `no differences were found for project $/xyz` notification. If you know there are differences, it probably means that you didn't define the Project Difference options dialog properly, or that it never appeared in the first place. You can toggle the visibility of the Project Difference option dialog by going to the Tools, Options menu, and from there, the Command Dialogs tab. You can turn on or off any of the dialogs that preface any of Visual SourceSafe's transactions.

The Difference for Project Dialog Box

Thus far in looking at differences, you've learned that there aren't that many "differences" between history and differences functions. That school of thought ends here, as you learn about the Difference for Project dialog. This dialog is a powerful means of listing the differences between a project and the working folder's contents, as well as navigating through those changes to get what you want. The functionality of the difference dialog borrows from many other aspects of Visual SourceSafe, as displayed in Figure 9.5.

FIG. 9.5
The Difference for Project dialog box—it does everything but the ironing.

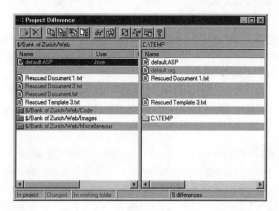

Now that you've seen all of those buttons, it's time to better learn how they can make your job easier, so you have more time to play games.

Understanding Project Difference Functions

All of the functions are found in buttons across the top of the display, and most should be familiar to you since they appear in other areas of Visual SourceSafe. In the File Differences dialog, the emphasis is on reconciling conflicts between two versions of a particular file. In the Project Differences dialog, this emphasis is changed to ensure that the project and the working folder's contents agree. The tools provided here reflect that goal, and their uses vary depending upon from which window pane you are selecting. Unlike the traditional Visual SourceSafe display, the left and right panes do not denote projects and files. The left pane is the Visual SourceSafe copy of whatever project you have selected. The right pane contains the contents of the working folder.

Table 9.1   General SourceSafe Functions in the Project Difference Dialog Box

Function	Definition
Add File	Adds the selected file to the project. In project difference parlance, adds the file to the left pane.
Delete	The delete function works as it always does in Visual SourceSafe if you use it in the left pane. If you delete a file or project in the right pane, it gives you the option of removing it from your hard drive.
Get Latest Version	Operates the same as it does in the Visual SourceSafe Explorer.
Check Out	Check Out performs its same operation, but has the added effect of moving the checked out file to the left pane, if it didn't already exist there. If the file were already in the working folder, then the check out reconciles any differences the two may have, since it replaces the working copy with the latest database copy.
Check In	Check In works as always, and in this case reconciles differences between files that vary between panes. Instead of overwriting the local copy as in Check Out, Check In takes the local copy and makes it gospel for the Visual SourceSafe database.
Undo Check Out	Will reconcile differences by replacing the current working folder copy with whatever the current VSS copy is.
View	The View command will bring up the default Visual SourceSafe viewer if used on an object in the left pane. If used on the right pane representing the working folder, VSS will call up whatever viewer is associated with that type of file.
Difference	If two files are selected, this command does a differences comparison on them. If only one is selected, the file is compared to its counterpart in the working folder (if any).
Reconcile All	This command attempts to reconcile all of the differences between the project and the working folder. It does so by selectively checking in, checking out, and deleting files, all of which you can control in the dialog box spawned by clicking this option.
Report	Generates a report detailing the project differences.

Part

III

Ch

9

All of these functions work as they usually do, but using them in the differences window makes you look at the bigger picture. Instead of checking files out to work on them, you're checking them out to make sure your working directory and your project listing match. The project differences tool is more for maintenance than creation, especially when trying to match up checked out projects to existing projects.

Back to Work

After his brush with unemployment, Jeff gets back to work with a vengeance. Unfortunately, he's been coasting for a while so his code is not up-to-date. Visual SourceSafe always keeps the most recent version, but Jeff knows that the underling programmers are working on the project right now.

Jeff uses the Project Difference utility to see what has changed and what has not by comparing the most recent copies of the Visual SourceSafe files to the copies in his working directory. He then reconciles his older copies by checking out new versions, all at once. He grimaces and internally realizes had he done this earlier, Jose might not have caught him slacking off. Hopefully he's now caught up enough to save his job.

Much as ancient shamans would forecast the future using animal entrails and marked sticks, you, too, need a special brand of skills to comprehend the listing you've just generated.

Understanding File Listings

Remember, this output has been filtered by the Project Difference options dialog. There may be files that do not appear in these listings because of the display options you have already set. Files are listed in certain colors or highlighted depending on their relationship to files in the project/working directory. Files that appear normally with black text on a white background are the same in both your project and working folder. You don't need to reconcile these files. File names with blue text on a gray background represent files that exist in your project, but not the working folder. If the background is gray, but the text color is green, it means that file exists in the working folder and not your project. This could be because a new file has been created and not added to the project, or the file was deleted from the project but not the working folder. Finally, file names that appear in red mean the file exists in both the project and working folder, but there are differences between the two.

Project Permissions

Like everything else in Visual SourceSafe, security is based around projects. If you have access to a project, you have access to all of the files in that project. The lowest divisible unit in VSS security is the project; you cannot restrict access to a particular file, you have to restrict the entire project itself. This means you have to be careful when assigning securities and designing project layouts. If you set it up correctly, Visual SourceSafe can operate as a security system as well as a revision control system.

▶ For more information about enabling security, **see** Chapter 12, "Visual SourceSafe Administration," on **p. 153**.

Visual SourceSafe has two basic levels of security: default and project.

Default Security

Default security has two possible settings: read-only and read-write. In default security you're either in or you're out, much like junior high school. Default security assignments are on a user-to-user basis, which means you can't allow specific access to specific projects. Project security allows for some deeper shades of meaning. The possible security assignments for project security are read, check out, add, and destroy. Project security is assigned to particular users and specific projects. This means that a user can have read access in one project, and check out access in another. You can't have one level of access without also inheriting all of the preceding security levels. Therefore, a user with destroy access would also have add, check out, and read access.

Read access permits users to simply look at files. You can't check them out or change them in any way. This is the rough equivalent to read-only access in default security. Check out access lets users edit and check in and out existing files. Add access allows you to add files to the Visual SourceSafe database. Finally, destroy access allows you to delete items from the Visual SourceSafe database. Destroy is the equivalent of read-write access in default security, and is the acme of VSS security access. People usually only get this far after rescuing the princess and beating the dragon. Remember that all of these access levels can be set on a project-by-project basis. You might have king of the hill status in one project, but you can't even check out files in another.

While easy to maintain and assign, default security lacks specificity. In order to achieve this you need to turn to the higher overhead of project security.

Project Security

Project security by default is hierarchical. If you have certain permissions to a project, those permissions propagate to the subprojects. The Administrator can change these settings at any time, but Visual SourceSafe automatically propagates your security permissions until told otherwise. The equation does not work backward though; if you have access to a subproject you do not automatically have access to its parent.

The main reason for enabling security is to keep people from where they don't belong. Whether this is because they're spies and saboteurs or just not supposed to be working there is irrelevant. Because you can't block access to a single specific file you need to be more careful when it comes to planning your project's layout. If there is one single file that only you should have access to, you have to put it in its own project. If you're using default security to try to protect that one file, you have to give everyone but yourself read-only access to the entire database. Not very efficient. Plan your projects completely, and if there are lots of high-security files, put them in the same project. That way you can keep track of them accurately instead of having several high-security areas with only one file in each area.

From Here...

You've learned a little more about the larger scope of Visual SourceSafe. The concept of an entire project suddenly becomes a small one when you are dealing with teams of people working on scores of projects. Not every company or organization will need this sort of power, but for those that do, Visual SourceSafe can be a boon. You can learn more about macro-managing projects in these chapters.

Chapter 10, "Backing Up Projects," teaches you what to do when the fickle finger of fate strikes, obliterating your Visual SourceSafe information. After all, you can't check out anything from something you can't boot up.

Chapter 11, "Using Multiple Databases," has all the information you need to set up and administer more than one database. It even tells you why you'd want to do such a thing.

Chapter 12, "Visual SourceSafe Administration," is the hidden chapter of power. Here you can learn all of the dark secrets that initiates into the forbidden Administrators guild learn. Plus, they get a nifty secret handshake.

CHAPTER 10

Backing Up Projects

No project is safe without a reliable method of storing your work. Almost everyone that uses a computer has experienced the "What do you mean the file is GONE?" syndrome. Now that you are counting on Visual SourceSafe day in and day out, you need to make sure that your data is safe and secure from harm. ■

"The Shadow knows..."

Shadow folders creep behind your every move, duplicating your work in case something happens. You should be happy about this.

Backing up, up and away...

Momma always said never leave all of your eggs in one basket (or something like that). Thrill and marvel in the simplicity of archiving your Visual SourceSafe database for more than posterity.

Using Shadow Folders

Shadow folders act as centralized folders on a server. These centralized folders contain the latest checked-in versions of your project files. Shadow folders, intended as a means of automated projects publishing, work ideally as a safety backup for your Web projects. If you have a separate server or destination directory to which you want your Web projects duplicated, using shadow folders simplifies the job. In the Visual SourceSafe Administrator, you can assign a shadow folder to any project, regardless of whether you have declared the project as a Web Project.

Why Would You Use Shadow Folders?

Shadow folders offer you a simple means of automated deployment. You could use them for:

- Deploying your Web site to an internal server for testing.
- Providing people on your team access to the Web files without needing to use Visual SourceSafe.
- Creating a duplicate of your project on a separate machine for backup purposes.
- Entertaining your friends and family at your next New Year's party.

Since the last option won't likely be your claim to fame, the others are discussed.

Deploying to an Internal Server   If you are working in a larger organization or with a team, you may find that it is easier to carry out your Web site testing on an internal server before deploying it. The quality assurance (QA) process of a Web site can involve a lot of changes and modifications until the product is up to standard. By using shadow folders to automate deployment of your Web files to an internal Web server, you can always make sure you are testing your most recent version. Once a file has passed your internal tests, you can then move on to deploying the site to the live Web server. By using this filtered approach to deployment, you are more likely to catch any possible problems before the site goes live.

Letting Your Co-Workers Have Access   Perhaps your co-workers need to preview all content before you publish it, but you're not using an internal Web server. By duplicating your Web Project files into a shadow folder, your teammates can have access to the files through local browsing. Although not as elegant or convenient as a local Web server, it still adds a layer to filter possible problems. This solution works best when you are dealing with static information and files.

Duplication for Backups   Losing work is never fun. The hours lost in attempts to recover your data, the justification to your boss and co-workers, and even worse: you may have to do the work again. Failure to keep backups is a recipe for disaster and one not likely to endear you to your employer. Visual SourceSafe enables you to create automated backups of your project through shadow folders. Shadow folders duplicate the latest versions of your project files to an assigned destination directory. Each time you carry out an edit on a file and check it in, SourceSafe scurries off into the background and duplicates your new file in the shadow folder.

Because your complete Web project is now present in the destination directory, it is safe in case of a catastrophic problem with your Visual SourceSafe database. You could opt to take the archival a step farther and perform backups of the shadow folder by using a tape drive, or similar device. If you ever need to recover your data from your backup, you can easily pull the files from the shadow folder and add them to the Visual SourceSafe database again.

Part
III

Ch
10

Jose and Shadow Folders: The Best of Friends

Jose was faced with a dilemma. Jeff's ongoing development with server-side programming for the Web site was resulting in crashes and continued problems for the test Web server. This translated into frustration and headaches for Marge, who was trying to keep up with demands for ongoing changes to the Web site. She could rarely test her site with the server consistently crashing, and she was usually forced to deal with Jeff while getting things fixed. This was never easy, and usually involved the butting of heads until Jeff would relent and fix the problem.

To solve the problem and speed up productivity, Jose placed a new machine into the local area network to function as a testing platform Web server for Marge. The existing server would remain for testing Jeff's code.

To mirror her working structure, Marge chose to use shadow folders to automatically deploy her most recent work to the test Web server. This allowed her to always see exactly what she was working on as she checked the files in. It just so happened that it also let Jose monitor her progress at the same time.

Setting Up Your Shadow Folder

Like Web Projects, shadow folders are defined using the Visual SourceSafe Administrator. In fact, the process is similar to defining Web Projects. You can easily set a project's shadow folder and forget about it. If you need to change the destination in the future, you simply modify the existing destination path within the Administrator. To set your project's shadow folder, follow these instructions:

1. Launch the Visual SourceSafe Administrator. If you currently have the Visual SourceSafe Explorer open, close it so that the changes to the database will take effect when you reopen it.

2. Choose Tools, Options to open the Options dialog box for the Administrator.

3. Select the Shadow Folders tab. This displays the shadow folder options, as shown in Figure 10.1.

FIG. 10.1
The Shadow Folders tab lets you set the destination for your project's shadow folder, as well as the shadow folder's files read-only attribute.

4. In the first text box, Set Shadow Folder for Project, you can enter the Visual SourceSafe path to the project you want to set up. You can also click the Browse button to use the graphical user interface to find the project.

5. In the second text box, Set Shadow Folder To, enter the destination path for your shadow folder. You can also click the Browse button to use the graphical user interface to find the destination directory. Your destination path may only be a local directory or a shared resource on your local area network.

6. Now that you have entered the project and destination path, you can alter how SourceSafe will place the files. By clicking the Set Read-Only Flag for all Files check box, you are write-protecting all the files that are copied into the shadow folder.

7. The End-of-Line Character for Files drop box lets you set what character will be used to end lines in each file. The default is a CR/LF (Carriage Return/Line Feed) combination. If your destination is a UNIX machine, you may need to change this setting.

8. The File Date/Time drop box lets you choose what time and date stamp the files will carry. The default is to use the current date and time for all copied files.

9. Now that you are done setting up your shadow folder, you can click the Set Another button to create another shadow folder, or click OK to close the Options dialog box. Save your changes.

Once created, Shadow folders do not require any intervention on your part. The process of updating the destination directory with the latest version is carried out automatically each time you check a file in.

N O T E Take note that creating a shadow folder for a project does not immediately copy the project's contents to the destination. This only occurs after you have checked in a file after editing it. If you want to copy all of your project's files at once, you should check out the project and then check it back in. ▪

Backing Up and Restoring Databases

The Visual SourceSafe database itself is a collection of files separated into directories on your hard disk drive. If anything happens to these files and directories, your SourceSafe database becomes corrupt and unusable. To protect your database from such a fate, you should carry out regular backups of your database. In the event of a catastrophe you will then be able to restore from your most recent backup, rather than lose all of your previous work. If you open your Visual SourceSafe directory on your hard disk drive (or on your network drive, if your database is located on a server) you will see a directory similar to the one shown in Figure 10.2.

FIG. 10.2

The Visual SourceSafe directory contains several subdirectories that hold the database. The most important subdirectory is the DATA directory; this is where the database is actually stored.

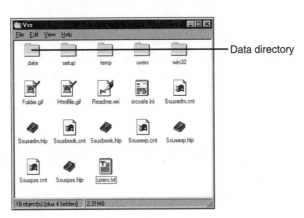

Data directory

The critical directory in backing up SourceSafe is the DATA directory and its subfolders. By fully archiving the DATA folder, you are backing up all of your projects and files, as well as their histories. In addition to the DATA folder, the USERS folder contains the user information for each Visual SourceSafe user you have created. This information is paired with the solitary USERS.TXT file found in the SourceSafe directory. When you are planning any backup, you should ensure that all of these are safely stored. Additionally, you should back up the two files named RIGHTS.DAT and STATUS.DAT. For simplicity's sake, you may want to back up your entire Visual SourceSafe directory.

Methods for Backing Up

When you choose to back up your Visual SourceSafe database, you can do so two ways:

- Use a backup device, such as a tape drive, to archive the Visual SourceSafe directories.
- Use an archival program such as WinZIP, to compress the Visual SourceSafe directories' contents. You then can copy the compressed file to another location.

Using a Backup Device   If you have a backup device, such as a tape drive, you can use specialized software for carrying out your backups. Most backup devices include backup software, as does Microsoft Windows NT (the backup software included in Windows 95 does not support tape drives). You may also choose to purchase third-party software for your backups, such as Seagate Backup (on the Web: **http://www.seagate.com**). Third-party software introduces many options the software doesn't offer, such as automated backups and extensive compression.

N O T E   When carrying out your backup using a tape drive or other backup device, always make sure you are doing a complete recursive backup and not an incremental backup. Because Visual SourceSafe already creates deltas for each file change, you want to provide yourself with a backup that you can fully restore and get back to work with. ■

Using a Compression Utility   If you are using a compression utility for your backup, you can easily carry out your backup from the comfort of the Windows Explorer. Using a compression utility such as WinZIP (on the Web: **http://www.winzip.com**), you should compress your complete Visual SourceSafe directory. You should ensure that you are carrying out a recursive compression to archive all of the folder's subdirectories, and that you are retaining the directory structure. To compress your directory using WinZIP, follow these instructions:

1. Open your Visual SourceSafe directory using the Windows Explorer. You may instead choose to launch WinZIP separately and position the windows so that you can easily access both windows. (If you have WinZIP menu shortcuts enabled, right-click the DATA directory, choose Add to Zip and skip to Step 4.)

2. Select the files you want to archive. To be safe, you may want to archive the entire Visual SourceSafe directory.

3. Drag the selected items into the WinZIP window. If you make a mistake, you can drag them one at a time.

4. The Add dialog box appears, as shown in Figure 10.3. This dialog lets you set the options for the compression. Click the New button to create a new archive in a destination directory. This button opens a Windows file dialog box to locate your destination and name your .ZIP file using the GUI. You may also specify the destination by typing it in.

Part

III

Ch

10

FIG. 10.3
WinZIP's Add dialog box lets you set the options for your new archive.

5. Make sure that the Action is set to Add (and Replace) Files. Set the compression to the level you desire.

6. Select the Recurse Folders check box to tell WinZIP to compress all of the files in the folder's subdirectories.

7. Click the Add button to add the selected items and compress them into your archive.

Your new .ZIP file is located in the assigned destination. The WinZIP dialog box lists all of the files and their paths. If you find that there is no path listed for all of your files, you did not set WinZIP to recurse directories. You need to go back and re-create your archive with this option selected. Now that your compressed archive contains your Visual SourceSafe database, you can safely copy your .ZIP file to its storage destination (if you have not already done so).

Jeff Causes Trouble: A Backup Story

Site Corporati had instituted a backup schedule right from the start of the project. Jose had clearly instructed all developers that all work was to be backed up daily, to minimize the impact of any potential loss. Because of the small development team, everyone needed to help out. Jose wrote up a schedule for the backups and labeled each tape. The last person out of the office each night was responsible for switching the tapes and initialing the schedule. It had worked fine until one night the unmentionable happened: a crash.

The main Visual SourceSafe database had been stored on a centralized server. The main hard disk drive failed late one night, resulting in the corruption of the database. After installing a new hard drive and preparing to restore the database from that night's tape, Jose was horrified to discover that Jeff had not switched the tape the night before. Even worse, he hadn't switched the tape any of the nights preceding the crash. Because he usually worked night hours, Jeff was responsible for switching the tapes but simply decided not to because he felt that would distract him.

Jose was furious. Thankfully, Marge still had her deployed copy from her test server, which saved the majority of all of the team's work. The data loss was minimal, but cost enough time and frustration that Jose quickly altered the backup schedule so that the first person in each morning would switch the tapes. This almost assuredly was Jose.

Restoring from Your Backup

Experience a disk failure? Computer blow up? Did industrial spies steal your Visual SourceSafe database? No worries, because you have your backup, right? Restoring your database from your archive is a simple effort. The exact restoration process depends on what method you used to back up your database.

If you used a tape drive or other backup device, you need to launch the backup software you used to archive Visual SourceSafe. Refer to the restoration instructions included with your software for specific information.

If you archived your Visual SourceSafe database using a compression utility such as WinZIP, you first need to extract your archive to uncompress all of the files and directories for your database. To restore your database from a .ZIP file, follow these steps:

1. Open your Visual SourceSafe directory using the Windows Explorer.

2. Open the directory containing your database archive and arrange it so that both windows are clearly visible.

3. If you have the WinZIP shortcut menus enabled, right-button drag your database archive into the Visual SourceSafe directory and choose Extract from the pop-up menu. If you do not have the shortcut menus enabled, go to Step 4.

4. If you have already extracted your archive, move on to Step 5. Otherwise, double-click the archive and choose Extract from within WinZIP; set your destination as the VSS directory.

5. Confirm that your DATA directory is properly extracted and located in your Visual SourceSafe directory.

N O T E You may discover two files missing when you restore your Visual SourceSafe database from a backup. Two files, RIGHTS.DAT and STATUS.DAT, are used by Visual SourceSafe to monitor the permissions of connected users. If you carried out your backup while someone was using Visual SourceSafe, you likely were not able to archive these two files.

The STATUS.DAT file is a small loss, as it will rebuild itself once Visual SourceSafe is run again. Unfortunately, the RIGHTS.DAT file requires more involved effort on your part to recover. The Analyze utility is used to check the integrity of your database and is included with Visual SourceSafe. This utility, which you must run as the Administrator, is covered in detail in Chapter 15, "SourceSafe Utilities."

A simple rule of thumb: make sure that no one on your team is using Visual SourceSafe while you create your backup. ▨

Part

III

Ch

10

Jose's Restoration

Using a combination of a week-old backup tape and the recovered files from the test Web server, Jose set out to restore the Visual SourceSafe database. After reinstalling the Visual SourceSafe software on the server, he uncompressed the files and carefully moved them to the Visual SourceSafe directory. After resharing the Visual SourceSafe directory, everyone could set back to work using SourceSafe. This time, however, everyone worked a little more cautiously and backed their files up a little more frequently.

From Here...

Backing up your Visual SourceSafe database is probably one of the smartest things you could do. Now that you know what there is to know about backing up and restoring databases, you're ready to move on:

■ Chapter 11, "Using Multiple Databases," is a short and sweet chapter on managing more than one Visual SourceSafe database. If you find yourself splitting your projects between different teams, you may want to look to more than one database.

■ Chapter 15, "SourceSafe Utilities," covers in detail the utilities included with Visual SourceSafe. This includes the Analyze utility that you read about earlier.

CHAPTER 11

Using Multiple Databases

Sometimes one database is just never enough. In working with Visual SourceSafe, you may find that you have too much data in one database for easy management. Or perhaps you have several different departments using Visual SourceSafe on different servers and you need to access each database from your workstation. Thankfully, Visual SourceSafe 5.0 introduced ease of use in handling multiple databases. ■

Why twins are better

For that matter, why not triplets? There are many advantages to using more than one Visual SourceSafe database dependent on your needs. You can play it safe and cramp your style with one database, or you can explore the options that numbers have to offer.

Cloning like a mad scientist

If you think of each Visual Source-Safe database as a laboratory, it makes sense to use more than one lab for large "experiments." SourceSafe helps you make these monster databases without your needing to summon an assistant.

Relearning for new additions

Just because you've created multiple databases doesn't mean everyone will be using them. You need to make sure that your teams connect to the new databases to start their work.

Advantages of Using Multiple Databases

By nature, Visual SourceSafe installations centralize all of your data into one database, rather than spreading it around in several different places. You might think that having all of your project files stored in one database is the best way to go, and on a whole, the world would be inclined to agree with you. Using one database is usually the preferred way of managing Visual SourceSafe data. However, as we all know, rules are sometimes meant to be broken. There are times when more is better than less.

Traditionally, single databases are used with Visual SourceSafe for a few reasons:

- With your data in one database, you can easily locate and manage your files. You don't need to open a separate database to find that nasty missing file.

- Multiple databases complicate sharing of data between databases. A direct Visual SourceSafe Share action is not possible. You usually have to use a command line utility to move files from one database to another.

- User information for Visual SourceSafe is unique to the database. This means that if you want to maintain more than one database, you have to make sure your users are set up in both databases.

Okay, so now you're totally turned off multiple databases, right? Why would you ever want to use one if these points are true? Sometimes there is a need for more than one database. Sometimes you are working in a large team setting, with a very large and diverse series of projects. Sometimes you may be working with many different teams that should never have access to the same machines on the network. Sometimes you're just into being difficult. These are valid (well, except maybe for the last) reasons for instituting multiple databases. Decentralization, or having autonomous development departments that don't rely on one another, is often a goal for many organizations.

Let's use an example. For brevity's sake, let's say that your company is as big as, well, Microsoft. You have a dozen teams working on different projects concurrently. Each team consists of ten to twenty developers, each working on its own assignments and using its own files. To complicate things even further, some of your development teams have access to certain network servers, others don't—all in the name of paranoid security and non-disclosure agreements. Why, in this case, would you want to have the developers use the same database?

It is true—you could have all of the teams operate in the same database, each with its own project trees. However, perhaps your teams never really need to share code between one another, aside from in e-mail, for instance? Would it make sense to leave the database on a communal server that needs the space to service all of these developers? Not necessarily.

It may be more plausible for you to implement team databases. These databases may even be shared with similar teams (Team 1, being unique, has its own database. However, Team 2 and Team 4 definitely do share a lot of files, so they may share a database).

If a decentralized development system is what you feel would be best for your teams, here are some considerations and advantages to using multiple databases:

- Multiple databases add that second level of security. Visual SourceSafe already provides a healthy set of access controls, but that second line adds an extra layer of security so that you can sleep easier at night.

- Multiple databases lower the group requirements for storage. Individual databases may be stored on smaller machines, even workstations, as opposed to a communal server that may require more resources.

- Multiple databases can provide better *up time*. In simple terms, in a centralized environment, nobody can work if your server goes down. In a decentralized environment, if one of the databases or servers go down, other teams can continue to work.

Multiple Databases Encroach on Site Corporati

As the FBoZ project grew, the amount of data in the SourceSafe database grew exponentially. Resource files, concepts and mocks, as well as the production files swelled the database and the organizational structure. To complicate the situation, several new developers had been brought in to pick up some of the slack from Jeff, as well as several new designers to work with Marge. This translated into more people accessing the SourceSafe database for disparate files.

Jose decided to move Marge's design group to a new SourceSafe database located on their test Web server, while leaving the existing database for the new developers and Jeff. Hopefully, Jose thought, this would speed things up and stop some of the bickering between Jeff and Marge regarding the structure of the SourceSafe database.

Setting Up Multiple Databases

Not content to remain with the status quo, you've decided to implement multiple databases. Jolly good for you! The Setup program during installation handles the actual Visual SourceSafe database construction. You create a fresh database, empty in all respects and ready for you to insert project files. That's all fine and well, but how do you make more than one? There is no direct facility for creating more than one database. When you want to create a second (or third, or fourth...) database, you must first identify how you want your Visual SourceSafe installation organized.

■ **Visual SourceSafe Databases on Separate Machines**. This is by far the simplest method for creating multiple databases. When first installing Visual SourceSafe using the server installation option, you create a usable database. There is no need for special tricks or copying because this is exactly how you are "supposed" to use Visual SourceSafe. This saves you from having to jump through hoops to create multiple databases, and is without a doubt the most reliable means of doing so. Each machine contains a unique database and acts as an isolated repository for your projects. If you have multiple machines at your disposal, you may find this the preferable method for expanding your databases.

■ **Visual SourceSafe Databases on the Same Machine**. This complicates things slightly more than your normal installation. Because you already have Visual SourceSafe set up and installed on your machine, you already have a database. How do you create a second one? Simple. Copy your current database into a different location. Remember how your SourceSafe database is simply a collection of different files in directories? That makes it easy to duplicate the contents to create a new database. This is best to do when the first database is blank. Your second option is to carry out a second install of Visual SourceSafe. If you install to a separate directory on your hard disk drive, then your current database won't be touched. Creating multiple databases on one machine requires more planning and consideration than creating them on separate machines. You must take care that each of your users is accessing the correct database and that security has been more thoroughly addressed.

Copying Your Existing Database

Do you remember in the previous chapter how you learned to back up your Visual SourceSafe database? That's right—all of the data itself is contained in the DATA directory (or folder, depending on your point of view and "tech" vocabulary). When you wanted to back your database up, you duplicated your database for safekeeping. In the case of creating a new database, you are copying your DATA folder for prompt and immediate change. Of course, if your database had something already in it when you duplicated it, you may need to remove the projects and files from the database once you're done. To duplicate your existing database, follow these steps:

1. Create a directory on your local hard disk drive where you want the new database stored. For example, D:\VSS2.

2. Using the Windows Explorer (or if you're a real adventurer, the command line), copy the Visual SourceSafe DATA directory into your newly created directory. In this example, you would copy the DATA directory to D:\VSS2\DATA.

> **CAUTION**
>
> Watch out! Make sure not to MOVE the files from your original DATA directory. You only want to COPY the files. If you accidentally MOVE the files, your original database will no longer work and you must move the files back in order to fix things.

3. Now that you have the database copied, you need to let Visual SourceSafe users see it. To do so, you must create a configuration file called SRCSAFE.INI (as shown in Figure 11.1). You can do this by opening the NotePad in Windows. Your new configuration file, to be stored in your new directory (D:\VSS), should read:

```
#include D:\VSS\SRCSAFE.INI
#Data_Path=DATA
```

Replace *D:\VSS* with the path to your existing Visual SourceSafe directory. This allows your new database to use the configuration settings from your first VSS installation. If you need your new database to have different settings than your original database, you can copy the entire SRCSAFE.INI file from your original VSS directory and modify it directly.

FIG. 11.1
The SRCSAFE.INI file contains the configuration information for Visual SourceSafe.

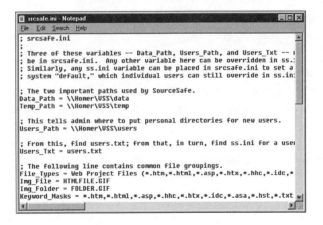

3. Just as when you first installed Visual SourceSafe, you need to create a Share for your new SourceSafe database. This will allow your SourceSafe users to access the new database on your network.

Adding a New Installation to the Same Machine

The main difference from your second installation of SourceSafe and your first on the machine is that you are not going to install it in the same place. Just as if you were copying your database to a new location, you want to make sure that the database is in a separate directory than the original installation. To add a new installation of SourceSafe to the same machine, follow these steps:

1. Run the Visual SourceSafe Setup program from your distribution media. Ensure that you are using a different destination directory than the original installation. For example, if your first installation is located in D:\VSS, place your second installation in D:\VSS2.

   ▶ **See** Chapter 2, "Getting Started," on **p. 19** for a refresher on using the SourceSafe Setup program

2. Share your new VSS database directory, just as you did in Chapter 2. To do so, use the Explorer to navigate to your new VSS database directory and right-click the icon. Choose Sharing to open the Sharing tab of the Properties dialog. Provide a share name for your users to connect with in the Share <u>N</u>ame text box and click OK.

3. Your new database can use the same settings as your original VSS database or use the defaults that were created for it. If you want your new database to use the same settings as your old database, replace the SRCSAFE.INI file in your new destination directory with the one listed in the steps (listed previously) for copying your existing database. If you do want your database to use its own settings, your database is ready to go.

Jose Makes Databases

Jose decided that the task of moving the existing design work into the new blank database would be prohibitive time-wise. Instead, he decided to duplicate the current database to the test Web server and allow Marge to remove the projects that did not pertain to her work. Because of the increased number of people using SourceSafe, Jose decided to have each installation use a unique setup and set of users. This kept problems to a minimum and security tight.

After duplicating the database, Jose removed Marge's work from the programmer's database. He also removed Marge from the list of users who could access the database. He then turned his attention to the new database, removing Jeff from the users. After adding the new users to both databases, Jose let Marge go to work. She reveled in removing Jeff's work—a sharp cackle could be heard from her office.

Using Multiple Databases from Visual SourceSafe Explorer

Your new databases are up and running. They're accessible from the network and your staff is eager to populate them. Now what do you do? Thankfully, Visual SourceSafe 5.0 makes it considerably easier to interact with multiple databases than previous versions did. Prior to version 5.0, every time that you wanted to work with a different database you needed to hand-edit your SRCSAFE.INI file before launching the Visual SourceSafe Explorer. Probably due to several whacks to the head, the Microsoft developers added in the new version a convenient means of opening databases from within the Explorer itself.

To open a different database from the Visual SourceSafe Explorer, do the following simple steps:

1. Once you've opened the Visual SourceSafe Explorer, choose File, Open SourceSafe Database.

2. Select a database. The available databases are listed in the Open SourceSafe Database dialog box, as shown in Figure 11.2. Available databases consist of SourceSafe databases to which you already have connected.

Part

III

Ch

11

N O T E If this is your first attempt to connect to another database, you should only see your original database. To locate other databases, click the Browse button. ■

FIG. 11.2

The Open SourceSafe Database dialog box lists available data-bases on the left.

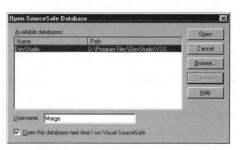

3. The Find Database dialog box, shown in Figure 11.3, is a standard Windows File Selector. It allows you to navigate your local directory structure or your network in order to find your new SourceSafe database. Find your new installation's SRCSAFE.INI and select it, then click OK.

FIG. 11.3
Almost every Windows user should be familiar with the Find Database dialog box.

4. The Username text box, shown previously in Figure 11.2, is where you enter the username you want to use with the database.

5. If you want this database to be opened the next time you use the Visual SourceSafe Explorer, click the Open this Database Next Time I Run Visual SourceSafe check box. This check box is located at the bottom of the dialog box shown in Figure 11.2.

6. Click the Open button, shown in Figure 11.2, to use the new database.

If you want to remove an available database from the list, select the database and click the Remove button. You will no longer see the database in the available databases list (but the database itself will be available again by browsing to it).

> **N O T E**   If you have chosen not to use auto-login for your SourceSafe installation, you are prompted for a password each time you launch the Visual SourceSafe Explorer. You can also use the Open SourceSafe Database dialog box to specify a different database by clicking the Browse button. ■

Setting Up Marge and Jeff

All that remained for Jose was to get both Jeff and Marge (as well as their teams) set up to access the appropriate database. Jose quickly went to the Web developers' workstations and browsed for their new database. Setting it as their default (to be opened the next time they launched the Visual SourceSafe Explorer), they were hooked up and ready to go. As a precautionary measure, Jose removed the old (now programmer) database from the list of available databases. It wasn't foolproof, but it was a deterrent.

With the Web developers ready to go, Jose double-checked all of the programmer's setups. They didn't require any modification, as they were already connecting to the proper database. When all was said and done, both teams could access their databases without any conflicts or problems. Jose smiled. He was pleased with the prospect of less bickering between Jeff and Marge. Patting himself on the back, he made a solemn oath not to hire argumentative employees ever again.

Maintaining Multiple Databases

The task of managing more than one database poses some interesting problems. First of all, data that you have put into one database is not directly available to another database. In its current form, Visual SourceSafe does not provide you with an easy means of moving projects and files to and from different databases. If you are faced with the need to share project files between databases, you have two options:

1. You can create the project and manually update each file in both databases when key changes occur.

2. You may manually archive the project and each file from the source database to a second database when key changes occur.

   ▶ **See** Chapter 15, "SourceSafe Utilities," on **p. 197** for complete details on archiving projects.

Neither of these two options is going to make you leap for joy and praise the ease of use, but you can carry out the duplication if the need arises. The general rule of thumb is that if you believe you will face sharing a lot of files between databases, don't. Use one database.

N O T E   Remember the cardinal rule with SourceSafe databases: projects were not meant to be shared between databases. Plan out your multiple database strategy and stick to your plan. If you think you're going to run into problems with multiple databases, it's time to go back to your plan and see if you really need more than one database. ▧

Removing Databases

There comes a time in every Administrator's life when he or she just has to say "Enough is enough." If you are faced with scaling back your Visual SourceSafe usage and no longer need multiple databases, you are faced with the task of deciding what to do with the poor database facing cutbacks. As mentioned previously, Visual SourceSafe does not provide you with any convenient means of migrating data between databases. If you do not need to move any data from the soon-to-be-retired database, you're in luck. All you need to do is delete your Visual SourceSafe directories and the deed is done. Of course, you need to update any of your users' machines to point to a new database, but all the same, the database is just a memory.

If you need to move your old data to a different database before euthanizing your old database, you need to make some plans. Like sharing content between databases, you have two options for moving your data:

1. You can manually GET your project's contents from your first database (the retiree), and then add the files to your surviving database.

2. Using the SSARC utility, you can archive your project files from the retiree database and restore the files into your surviving database.

   ▶ **See** Chapter 15, "SourceSafe Utilities," on **p. 197** for more information on the SSARC utility and archiving projects.

From Here...

Now that you've mastered the "simple" skills of Visual SourceSafe, you're ready to tackle the real meat and step into the Advanced Topics.

- Chapter 12, "Visual SourceSafe Administration," gives you the almighty power of being SourceSafe Administrator. Discover the inner secrets of the ever-present Administrator tool.

- Chapter 15, "SourceSafe Utilities," leads you down the twisty path of supplementary programs. These utilities, included with your Visual SourceSafe software, fulfill several roles.

- Chapter 16, "Cross-Platform Usage," jumps you into dealing with more than one operating system. Working on a Mac? Don't worry, you won't be mocked. In fact, this chapter helps you deal with the ever-present cross-platform compatibility issues.

Exploring Advanced Topics

CHAPTER 12

Visual SourceSafe Administration

No exploration of Visual SourceSafe would be complete without detailing the seedy underbelly of Visual SourceSafe and the denizens of the VSS underdark: The Administrator. As the Visual SourceSafe Administrator (the person, not the program), it is your responsibility to organize and maintain the SourceSafe installation for all users. You set the options and the tone for all users of SourceSafe. You, effectively, have the power to control how the other users work. To carry out your righteous task, your primary tool will be the Visual SourceSafe Administrator (the program, not the person). ■

Master of your own molds

One file format is never enough. Your Web site is brimming with project files and content, all neatly stacked and ordered. But wait! A new program? A new type of file? How ever will you make SourceSafe recognize what this new thing is? File types to the rescue!

Under tight lock and key

Keep your projects in the closet, away from prying eyes. Visual SourceSafe provides you with the ability to decide who's too cool for school, and lock them out. If only grade school were this fun.

Projects of the Web kind

You've explored the role of Web Projects before, but now it's time to get down to the nitty-gritty. Explore the seamy world of Web projects and how they may just save your life.

Skulking in the shadows

Shadow folders aren't just for back-ups. Cast some illumination on the whole shadow debacle and get the real scoop on these dark projects.

Project File Types

Not all files are created equal. That is likely the case with most Web developers. You assign a greater importance to certain types of files, usually your Web pages themselves (HTML) and the images that they use (all those nasty graphic formats). The rationale behind this is simple: as a Web developer, you may not really care about certain file types for your projects. You only want to deal with those files that are important to your work and have a direct bearing on your project. Makes sense. Aside from this reason, you may also want to group your files to control how Visual SourceSafe manages them.

Because you can store essentially any kind of data in your SourceSafe database, it stands to reason that certain functions of SourceSafe won't work with all of the possible data. Certain features of SourceSafe only work with *text* files, such as your Web pages coded in HTML. For example, merges and multiple checkouts can only be carried out on text-based files because it could be disastrous if Visual SourceSafe tried to merge changes made to a graphic file altered by seven people. This is most visible when you try to view the differences in a binary file, where you can only see that the file has changed and cannot see the changes themselves.

Visual SourceSafe also lets you group similar file types into logical groupings. You can then instruct SourceSafe to recognize certain groups or files as binary files. This also provides you with a convenient method of organizing your file types. This can tremendously simplify the task of adding files to your projects. By establishing file groups of, say, all graphic formats, you can filter the files in a directory to display on files in a certain group. The groupings you create appear as file selection filters in the List Files of Type edit box, at the bottom of the Add Files dialog box. You can see this dialog box in Figure 12.1.

FIG. 12.1
By using file type groups, you can filter out files from the Add Files dialog box.

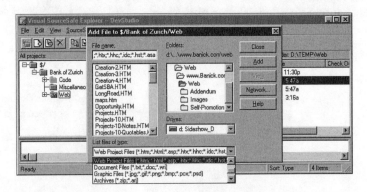

Adding and Removing File Types

Your co-workers will be amazed at how easily you can modify the SourceSafe file types. You'll be the center of attention at the office, and don't be surprised if you are asked to appear on one of those late night infomercials you always stayed up to watch. If you have already explored the Visual SourceSafe Administrator's Options dialog box, you no doubt have stumbled upon the File Types tab, as shown in Figure 12.2. Notice that the text box for defining binary file types is at the top and all file type groups are listed in the large box in the center of the dialog.

FIG. 12.2

The File Types tab in the Options dialog box is where you get down to work.

The File Types tab has three fields: Binary files, File groups, and File types. The top field is the <u>B</u>inary Files text box. Normally, when you add a file to your Visual SourceSafe project it carries out an automatic detection of the file type. This detection isolates the file either as a text file or a binary file. By specifying file types in this text box, you are telling Visual SourceSafe to always treat those files as binary files and skip the autodetection. You can choose an Advanced option to override the autodetection in the Add File dialog box.

The second and largest field is the <u>F</u>ile Groups listing. On the left is a list of all groupings and on the right are the <u>A</u>dd and <u>D</u>elete buttons. By default, Visual SourceSafe contains file groups for Relevant Masks (this displays all files using the infamous *.* wild card), Microsoft Visual C++, Microsoft Visual Basic, and Visual FoxPro. When you click a group, the third region of the dialog box comes into play.

The bottom field, File <u>T</u>ypes Included in the File Group, lists the extensions of each file type for the selected grouping. Notice that a comma separates each file type.

To add a file type group, follow these steps:

1. Click the Add button.

2. The Add File Group dialog box, shown in Figure 12.3, lets you enter a name for the new file group. Choose something descriptive, such as "Graphic Files," to fine-tune your Add File tasks easily.

FIG. 12.3
The Add File Group dialog box lets you specify a name for your new file group.

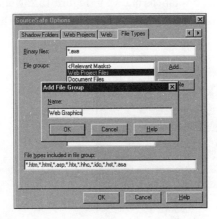

3. Enter the file extensions for your file types in the bottom text box, with each extension separated by a comma.

4. If you want to add another file group, repeat the process. Otherwise, click the OK button to commit your changes and close the Options dialog box.

CAUTION
You can delete a file type group by selecting the group from the list and clicking the Delete button. Beware, however—you cannot undo this action, and there is no confirmation.

Modifying Existing Groups

As you work, you may find yourself adding and removing types of files from your workload. It makes sense that you may want to change your file type groups in SourceSafe as well. Editing an existing group couldn't be much easier. In fact, it's so simple that you may not want to tell your boss. Be creative, make it sound complex. To modify a group, follow these steps in the Options dialog box, under the File Types tab:

1. Select the group you want to modify from the list.

2. In the bottom text box, modify the extensions for the file types, keeping in mind each file type must be separated by a comma.

3. Once you are satisfied with your changes, click the OK button to close the Options dialog box and commit your changes.

Unfortunately, you cannot change the name of a group once you have created it. If you find yourself desperately wanting to change the group you named "The Stupid Boss' Files" to save your job, you need to re-create the group. It's a quick task.

1. Select the file types from your original group and hit Ctrl+C to copy them into the clipboard.

2. Add the new group with the new and proper name.

3. Paste the clipboard contents into the bottom text box using Ctrl+V.

4. Once you're done, you can safely remove the old group by deleting it.

N O T E By establishing file type groups from the Visual SourceSafe Administrator, you are setting the standard file types for all users who work with the database. If individual users find themselves needing several different file types, you can save yourself some work by letting them create and modify their own file type groups from the Visual SourceSafe Explorer. Identical in appearance to the File Types tab in the SourceSafe Administrator's Options dialog box, the File Types tab in the Explorer's Options dialog box lets users set their own types. These changes only are effective for that user, and do not in any way affect your SourceSafe database. ▪

Jose Establishes the File Trend

The Site Corporati team was already dealing with a large number of file types for the SourceSafe database. Between Marge's Web development files (comprised of .HTM and .ASP files for Web pages, .JPG and .GIF image files, and several .WAV sound files) and Jeff's programming work (all of his C++ code, include files, pre-compiled headers, and the like), the database was filled with somewhere near a dozen different file types. Each developer would consistently gripe about having to filter out unrelated file types in his or her SourceSafe actions, especially when adding files.

To alleviate these concerns, Jose dug into the Visual SourceSafe Administrator and set out to create several groups of files specific to their type. He grouped graphic and HTML files into separate groups for Marge, as well as the many different programming files for Jeff. For himself, he added a group with a few file types for extra documents he had placed in the database for safekeeping. By the end, Jose had six different groups: HTML (.HTML, .HTM, and .ASP files), Graphics (.GIF, .JPG, .BMP, .PSD, and .TIFF files), Executables (.EXE and .COM files), Source Code (.C, .H, .OBJ, .MAK, and .OBJ files), General Documents (.TXT, .DOC, and .WRI files), and finally, a Miscellaneous group (.BAT, .INF, and .INI files), for files they infrequently modified.

With the file types in place, Jose found less bitter griping from the developers and even found it easier to locate his own documents in the database.

Security

The last thing anybody wants is for that irritating guy in the office to get access to the Web site. Next thing you know, he'd have the site plastered with advertisements for *Joseph and the Amazing Technicolor Dreamcoat* or the newest low-rated show on FOX. Security is an important aspect of any business. You always want to make sure that your work can't be tampered with, and that it is always safe from prying eyes. Visual SourceSafe provides several ways of controlling how people access your SourceSafe database. Visual Source-Safe security works very similarly to UNIX file system rights. As an Administrator, you can control who can read a file, who can modify a file (as opposed to execute under UNIX), and who can delete a file. Although not identical, if you are familiar with UNIX security, you should find SourceSafe security very comforting.

Restricting access is even more important when you have several individuals and teams working on separate projects. For several reasons, you may not want certain teams to be able to see (or modify) what another team is working on. Thankfully, Visual SourceSafe has the ability to outright stop someone from entering Visual SourceSafe without the appropriate "credentials," as well as limit what specific users can access within the database.

User and Project Access Rights

Controlling who does what in Visual SourceSafe gets down to *who* is accessing *what*. The *who*, in this case, is the user. The *what* is the project. To access the Visual SourceSafe database you must connect as a user. The user's name can be the same as his or her network username (assigned by system administrator) used to log into your workstation, or something uniquely different. In fact, users don't have to be "users," per se. A user for Visual SourceSafe could be an entire team, all sharing the same username. This defeats the purpose of tracking individual changes by each user, but it can be done, nonetheless. The main idea behind a user is to identify exactly who is interacting with the Visual SourceSafe database.

As you learned earlier in the book, projects represent the collection of files for your work. With this in mind, you can look upon projects as being similar to a room. Each room contains several articles. You may want to lock the room to prevent anyone from entering unless they have key privileges. Visual SourceSafe lets you assign a series of keys to users. One key may let your users enter the room, another may let them open a cabinet containing files once they are inside the room. Essentially, you can restrict what users can do to your projects by limiting what keys they have. You have several keys, or "rights," available to you:

■ *Read*. By giving a user the Read key, you are allowing him or her to open and view any files within a project. The user can't alter the files in any way, but can view them within Visual SourceSafe. Read rights also include the ability for your users to see lists of files. If a user selects a project that he or she does not have Read permissions for, the project appears blank.

■ *Check Out/Check In*. The Check Out/Check In key lets your user utilize Visual SourceSafe's library services. This lets the user check the file out, edit and modify it, and then check the file back in. If you want your users to actually work with Visual SourceSafe, this is the key they need most.

■ *Add/Rename/Delete*. Users that can change the name of a file inside a project, remove a file from a project, and add new files to the project require the Add/Rename/Delete key. By giving this right to your users, you are allowing them to directly modify the project itself and not only the files. You must also have this right if you want to label a project.

■ *Destroy*. Deleting a file from a project does not actually destroy the file. Instead, when you delete a file inside Visual SourceSafe, you are placing it in a "safety bin" for the project. You can save the file from the safety bin at any time, until you purge the bin. The ability to purge files or projects relies on the Destroy key. When you have this right, you are able to permanently remove a file from the Visual Source-Safe database. Once you destroy a file, it is not recoverable. This key involves the commands of Destroy, Purge, and Rollback. You should only give this key to Administrators and project leaders.

User rights come in the same order as listed. For example, if you want your user to have the ability to Add files to a project, that same user must have the Check In/Check Out right. To take the example further, a user cannot have the Destroy right without the preceding rights.

Enabling Project Security   By default, Visual SourceSafe lets any of your users carry out any action. To limit the rights of your users, you must first flip the switch on project security. Enabling project security is like telling Visual SourceSafe to post guards at each entry point in the database. Whenever one of your users tries to carry out an action on the database, these guards check their credentials. If your user has the rights to do that action, the guards let them past to do their work. If your user does not have the right keys, the guard cries "Halt!" and the process is stopped before anything can be done. Imagine that—your own little police force.

To enable project security, you should follow these steps:

1. Launch the Visual SourceSafe Administrator and open the Options dialog box. This is done by choosing Tools, Options.

2. Switch to the Project Security tab as shown in Figure 12.4. Here, you can also set the default keys for all users.

FIG. 12.4

Control project security by setting the default keys for all users.

3. Select the Enable Project Security check box. The list of four check boxes becomes available to you.

4. Select the check boxes for the user rights you want to make default. When you choose a right from these check boxes, you are making this right available to all users. You can edit specific users' rights if you want to deviate from the defaults.

5. Click the OK button to close the Options dialog box and commit your changes.

Now that you have specified the default security rights for users, each new user you create for Visual SourceSafe will have these rights.

Assigning Rights by Project   With project security enabled, you can do more than set the basic rights of all users. Visual SourceSafe also provides you with the ability to assign users' rights on a project-by-project basis. The simple rationale to this is that some of your users may require different permissions for different projects. The first method of customizing rights is by doing so on a Project basis. Visual SourceSafe calls this *Assigning Rights by Project*. Using this method, you can control which of your users can access the project and in what capacity.

Rights by Project displays all of the users who have rights in a project, as well as the effects of *rights propagation*. Rights propagation works on the model of a hierarchical flow chart. If you give your users rights on a project, those same rights are carried down into its subprojects. For example, you have created a project named $/RootWeb and have given your user the ability to Read (R), Check In/Check Out (C), and Add/Rename/Delete (A). You also have a subproject of $/RootWeb called $/RootWeb/Data. The same rights (R, C, and A) you provided your user apply to the subproject. If you wanted your user to have differing rights for the subproject (in this case, $/RootWeb/Data), you would have to specifically set the permissions for the user in that subproject.

To control your Rights by Project, follow these steps:

1. While in the Visual SourceSafe Administrator, choose Tools, Rights by Project from the menu bar.

2. The Project Rights dialog box, as shown in Figure 12.5, appears. The left side of the dialog box displays a tree-like list of your SourceSafe database's projects. Select the project for which user rights must be modified.

FIG. 12.5

The Project Rights dialog box displays all of the projects in your SourceSafe database in the left-hand window pane.

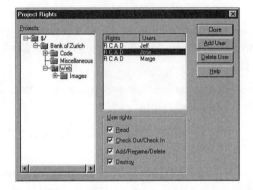

3. Select a user whose security rights you want to modify. Having selected a project from the left, the list on the right changes to reflect the user rights for the project. Each of your users that has access to the project is listed, as well as his or her security rights. Rights are listed by a letter: R for Read, C for Check In/Check Out, A for Add/Rename/Delete, and D for Destroy.

4. With a user selected, choose the appropriate rights for the user from the four check boxes below the list. Keep in mind that the rights rely on one another.

5. If the user should not have any rights to the project, you can remove the user from the project entirely. To do so, select the user and click the Delete User button. Your user is still available in the SourceSafe database, but is restricted from entering this project. You are asked to confirm the deletion of this user from your project. If you're sure, click Yes.

6. If you have a user who should have access to your project and does not appear in the list, you can add the user to the project. Click the Add User button to open the Add Users dialog box, as shown in Figure 12.6.

Part
IV

Ch
12

FIG. 12.6

In the Add Users dialog box, you can add more than one user at once by holding down the Ctrl key and selecting each user.

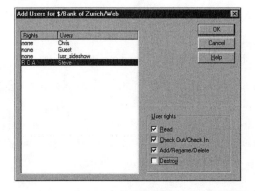

7. Select the user (or users) you want to add to your project. Before adding the user, you can select the user's security rights by using the four familiar check boxes on the right.

8. Click the OK button to add the user (or users) to your project. The new user(s) now appears in the list of users for your project.

9. Once you are done modifying your projects, click the OK button to close the dialog box and commit your changes.

Assigning Rights for Users   The previous method of controlling user security rights is considerably more project-centric than some workplaces need to be. Often it is easier to look at things on a user-by-user basis. This is the idea behind the Assignments for User method of controlling security in Visual SourceSafe. When you choose to modify rights in this fashion, all projects in which your user has rights are displayed. Visual SourceSafe refers to this as an *assignment*. The rights of your user in the assigned projects are listed, but the effect of rights propagation is not displayed. You can use the Rights by Project dialog box to view this.

To modify security rights on a user-by-user basis, follow these steps:

1. From the Visual SourceSafe Administrator, select the user you want to edit from the user list.

2. Choose Tools, Rights Assignments for User. The Assignments dialog box appears, as shown in Figure 12.7.

3. Select the project for which you want to edit the user's rights. Projects to which you have assigned the user are listed in the bottom half of the dialog box. The user's rights in the project are listed in the left of the list.

4. Using the four familiar check boxes in the top left, modify the user's rights to the selected project. Keep in mind the order of the security rights.

FIG. 12.7

The Assignments dialog box lists each of the projects in which the user has permissions to work.

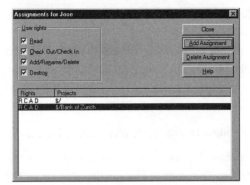

5. Select the project and click the <u>D</u>elete Assignment button if you want to remove a user's assignment to a project entirely. The project is no longer accessible by your user.

6. Click the <u>A</u>dd Assignment button if you need to assign your user to a project that does not appear in the list. The Add Assignment dialog box appears, as shown in Figure 12.8.

FIG. 12.8

The Add Assignment dialog box lists a tree-like view of the projects in your SourceSafe database.

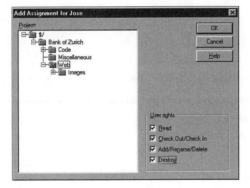

Part
IV

Ch
12

7. On the right is a list of the projects in your Visual SourceSafe database. Select the project you want to add as an assignment for your user.

8. You can directly specify the security rights for the selected project by using the <u>U</u>ser Rights check boxes in the lower right of the dialog box.

9. Click the OK button. You can see the new assignment in the list for your user.

10. Once you are done modifying your user's assignments, click the OK button to close the dialog box and commit your changes.

Copying Other Users' Rights   There comes a time when it is inconvenient to edit each user by hand, especially if you are in a rush. As a time-saving feature, Visual SourceSafe provides you with the Copy User Rights ability. This lets you use one user as a template and copy his or her access rights to another user. This is ideal if you are working with teams that have similar access rights. After the copy, the two users have functionally identical rights. If you need to deviate from the copy at any time, you can use the other methods of controlling access rights to edit a user. Your changes are not copied to another user unless you choose to copy his or her rights again.

The steps involved in copying user rights are as follows:

1. In the Visual SourceSafe Administrator, select the user you want to use as the template for your copy. This user will be the destination for the copy.

2. Select Tools, Copy User Rights. The Copy Rights Assignments dialog box, shown in Figure 12.9, appears.

FIG. 12.9

The Copy Rights Assignments dialog box lets you select the user as the template for your copy.

3. Select the user that has the access rights you want to duplicate. This user will be the template for the copy.

4. Click the OK button to commit the copy. The access rights for the template are copied to the destination.

Jeff Gets into Trouble

Sad but true—Jeff fancies himself a Web designer. He often opened Marge's work and "improved it," only to have Marge screaming at him in a startling fashion. One late night, Jeff noticed one of the Web developers had not logged out of Visual SourceSafe. Pleased with himself, he started to comb through the Web developer's SourceSafe database to see how things were taking shape. He made a few changes here and there, thinking no one would care. After all, he was a designer, too.

The next day Marge came in to find Jose in a panic. He had come in early to deploy the Web site for a demonstration to the bank people, only to find that large portions of the site didn't work. Not only that, somehow one of the Web developers had edited several key files when the developer wasn't even in the office. Jose had rolled the files back to a functional version, but he was insistent that there had been a security hole somewhere.

Marge knew what the deal was; she had seen it before. She could smell Jeff's lingering programmer's stench in the Web development office. She persuaded Jose to talk to Jeff about the mysterious edits, while she used Jose's SourceSafe Administrator to set up more stringent security. Some of the developers, including the hapless developer who did not log out, did not need access to the more crucial areas of the Web site. The other developers were only here to do the more menial layout work. She quickly restricted the developers from several key areas, ensuring that nothing like this could happen again on one of Jeff's late night work sessions.

Locking Databases

There comes a time in every Administrator's life when he or she has to lock everyone out of their work and inconvenience productivity. The Visual SourceSafe Administrator lets you lock all users out of the SourceSafe database for just such an occasion. You usually want to lock the database when you are running a utility on the database, backing up the database, or when you are upgrading Visual SourceSafe. When you lock the database, no one will be allowed to log into the database regardless of how nice they are or what kind of cookies they bake for you. The users who have already logged into the database are unaffected by your locking the database, so you are forced to manually convince them it is in their better interest to log out.

To lock your Visual SourceSafe database, follow these steps:

1. From the Visual SourceSafe Administrator, choose Tools, Lock SourceSafe database.

2. The Lock Visual SourceSafe dialog box, shown in Figure 12.10, lists the users who are currently logged into the database. You need to kindly ask these users to log out before you carry out your administrative tasks on the database. Select the Lock all Users Out of Visual SourceSafe check box to lock the database to prevent others from logging in.

Part
IV

Ch
12

FIG. 12.10
When you lock your SourceSafe database, you are preventing users from connecting. You still have to ask currently active users to disconnect.

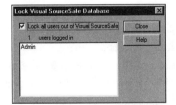

3. Click the OK button to commit your change.

4. Once you have completed your administrative tasks, reopen the dialog box and deselect the Lock all Users Out of Visual SourceSafe check box. Your users can once again log into Visual SourceSafe and hopefully get back down to work.

Jose and the Lock Down

Because everyone in the Site Corporati office except Jeff works during the day, Jose usually likes to run the backups in the mornings. The routine is predictable—Jose arrives early in the morning and sits down to read his mail. Before he does so, he usually pops a new tape into the server and starts a backup on the database. The whole task is usually done before anyone else steps foot into the office. Unfortunately, some of the new developers have been coming in earlier than expected and logging into Visual SourceSafe just as Jose starts the backup. Because users had logged into the database, some files could not be archived to tape because they were in use. To solve the problem, Jose now locks the database first thing in the morning, preventing the developers from logging in. He quickly starts the backup and archives the database to tape. Once he is done, he unlocks the database and the developers can get back to work.

Web Projects

In Chapter 6, "Deploying Content," you first learned about creating Web Projects. Never one to rest on simple coverage, you're now ready to jump into everything you ever wanted to know about Web Projects (and then some). As mentioned in Chapter 6, Web Projects are a way of representing complete Web sites within a Visual SourceSafe Project. Sort of like special citizens, these projects stand out amongst the crowd of everyday, "commoner" projects. Don't get smug, your special Web Projects haven't distinguished themselves yet.

A Project by any Other Name...

Previous versions of Visual SourceSafe have been geared toward programmers. Oh sure, you could put almost any kind of file into SourceSafe and it would happily chug along and do its thing, but all the same Visual SourceSafe was meant for the management of source code. With the advent of the World Wide Web and its growing popularity, ingenious little Web developers began to see Visual SourceSafe as an option for their own development projects. No doubt, these same Web developers had exposure in the programming arena to recognize the potential of SourceSafe.

Visual SourceSafe was workable for Web developers but required a few extra steps. For example, whenever you wanted to publish your site, you had to copy the site to your Web server. This was simple if you were working on a local area network, the standard GET feature accomplished the publishing with little effort. However, if you were publishing to a remote server via FTP, you had considerably more work to do. You were forced to first GET your project into a directory, so that all of the files were up-to-date, and then manually FTP the files into the appropriate location on your Web server. No automation, no fun.

In addition to the publishing conundrum, you had to manually keep track of what files were being published, what files changed, and what linked to what. Now, this isn't anything new to Web developers, but isn't the whole idea of a new tool to make your job easier? In many ways, Visual SourceSafe did just so, but it lacked in other areas due to its programmer-centric background.

Then came SourceSafe 5.0. The world smiled, the birds sang, and Web developers everywhere had tears of joy streaming from their eyes. Perhaps a little melodramatic, but all the same, the essential enhancements in this new release were addressed to Web developers and Web developers alone. Functionally, very little had changed from version 4.0 to version 5.0. Instead, Microsoft chose to address some of Visual SourceSafe's shortcomings for Web developers, recognizing an entirely new market. The most important change was the introduction of Web Projects.

Web Projects represent a slightly different way of looking at projects. In the past, all projects were essentially equal and were not distinguished differently from other projects in any way. Web Projects introduced the concept of *classed projects*. Much like differing families of fruit, now projects had their own diversity. Web Projects on their own are not much different than standard projects, but coupled with the new Web-oriented features of Visual SourceSafe, they prove valuable to Web developers (and programmers still don't see what the fuss is about). Who knows what project types could be included in future versions of Visual SourceSafe?

Part
IV

Ch
12

Web Projects Revisited

When you create a project inside Visual SourceSafe, you are creating a container for all of your work. SourceSafe itself doesn't care what you do with the project, or what you fill it with. With the exception of file types for addition and keyword expansion, SourceSafe is deaf, mute, and blind to what content you put in your project. Web Projects add some intelligence to standard SourceSafe projects. Not a lot—your Web Project won't do your taxes or wash your car, but it adds just enough to solve some of the dilemmas faced by Web developers when using SourceSafe.

First off, Web Projects care about your content. They really do. To prove it, you can use the SourceSafe Verify Links feature. As you learned in Chapter 6, the process of validating your links manually can be tedious and error-prone. Web Projects allow Visual SourceSafe to verify that each internal link in your file (be it a page, a graphic, a sound file, whatever) is present. In doing so, you can't say you are surprised by any dead links when you go to publish.

Second, Visual SourceSafe treats deployment with Web Projects in a kinder, gentler fashion than standard projects. As you learned in Chapter 6, deployment is simple with the ability to directly publish your Web site to a LAN server or a remote FTP server without any extra steps. The addition of automatically generated site maps certainly doesn't hinder making things easier.

The Web Projects Tab Having learned how to quickly create a Web Project, you now explore in more detail the options available to you in the Web Projects tab from the SourceSafe Options dialog box. By choosing Tools, Options from the Visual SourceSafe Administrator menu bar, the Options dialog box appears, as shown in Figure 12.11.

FIG. 12.11
Use the Web Projects tab to classify your project as a Web Project and take advantage of the new Web-oriented features.

This dialog box is straightforward and offers you a few areas for text entry. In closer detail, these are the elements of the dialog:

- This Project Represents a Web Site. The top text box is where you enter your Visual SourceSafe project's path. This is entered in the form of $/Project. You may optionally use the Browse button to use the graphical user interface to choose your SourceSafe project. Once you have selected a project, the remaining text boxes in the dialog box become editable.

- URL. The second text box lets you provide the *Universal Resource Locator* for your Web project. Prefixed with the familiar http:// for a Web site, you should enter your Web site's server address. You do not need to enter the subdirectory in this text box; that can be entered in the third text box.

- Virtual Root. If your Web site is accessible from a subdirectory of the root Web server, you should specify the virtual root in the third text box. For example, if your Web site is accessed from the address of http://www.server.com/mysite, your virtual root would be entered as `mysite`. You do not need to enter the preceding slash.

- Site Map Filename. By default, Visual SourceSafe's site maps are created using the file name SITEMAP.HTM. If you want to use a different file name, enter the complete file name in the fourth text box of the dialog box.

- Deployment Path. The final text box is the do-or-die text box—your destination for your publishing. Your deployment path may be a local hard disk drive path (C:\ InetPub\WWWRoot, for example), a local area network path (\\Server\WWW Root), or an FTP URL (ftp://www.server.com). You can use the Browse button to use the graphical user interface to locate your local or LAN directory path. For FTP URLs, you can enter a username and password to use for connecting. To do so, enter them in the format of: ftp://username:password@www.server.com.

- Set Another. Done setting up your Web Project? Ready to do another? To do so, click the Set Another button. This commits your new Web Project to the database and clears the dialog box, preparing it for you to start a new project.

The Web Tab   In addition to the Web Projects tab, Visual SourceSafe provides the Web tab in the Options dialog box. This tab is used to control how your Web Projects are deployed when dealing with a remote server. This is of the utmost importance if you are working in a company behind a *firewall*, which prevents open access to the Internet.

N O T E   A *firewall* acts as a barrier between the Internet and a company's internal network. Used to prevent unauthorized access to the local area network from the Internet, a firewall can often pose a problem for users who are trying to access the Internet. To connect to the Internet from inside the LAN, users most commonly go through a gateway called a *proxy*. Proxy servers act as an intermediary between the LAN and the Internet. A user on the LAN requests an action to be carried out on the Internet and passes that request to the proxy server. The proxy server then determines if the user has the access rights to do so. If the user does, the proxy then carries out the action on the Internet for the user, returning the information to the user. If the user does not have sufficient access rights, the proxy informs the user and the request never enters the Internet. See the fields in Figure 12.12, in which you must enter information to control the user's Web access. If you are deploying to the Internet from behind a firewall, you should consult your network administrator for proxy information. ■

Part

IV

Ch

12

FIG. 12.12

The Web tab is used to specify a proxy server on your network.

The Web tab is very simple, comprised of just three text boxes:

- <u>P</u>roxy for Deploying Over FTP. If you are working with a proxy server on your LAN, you must enter its address here. Depending on how your local area network is configured, you may be forced to enter the IP (numbered) address to your proxy server instead of its *fully qualified domain name* (named) address.

- <u>D</u>o not Use the Proxy Server for These Local Servers. If you enter a proxy server address in the first text box, the second text box becomes editable. When you are deploying content to a local area network server for testing, you likely would not want to involve the proxy server. You can enter the network address (either the IP or named address) for any local servers in this text box. If you are entering more than one server, separate them with a comma.

- Default <u>F</u>ilename for Web Pages. This text box lets you specify the file name that Visual SourceSafe appends to an URL that ends in a folder name. This comes into play when you carry out link verification. By default, Visual SourceSafe uses the file name DEFAULT.HTM. You should specify a different file name if your needs differ.

Jose Revisits Web Projects

Jose hadn't read the Microsoft documentation very closely when he began using Visual SourceSafe. He was never really all that clear on what Web Projects did, but all that mattered was that they worked. One day Marge began to complain that she was getting a lot of link verification errors that shouldn't be occurring. Sure that it wasn't in her work, she pestered Jose to check the Visual SourceSafe Administrator to make sure her project had properly been set up as a Web Project.

Much to his surprise, Jose discovered he had entered an incorrect virtual root path in the Web Projects tab, as well as an incorrect default file name in the Web tab. When Visual SourceSafe

went to verify Marge's links, any link that ended in a folder name resulted in an error. Visual
SourceSafe was looking for the wrong file—the one entered by Jose in the Web tab, rather than
the one Marge had created with the correct name.

Embarrassed by his error, Jose quickly fixed the problem and promised to buy Marge lunch.

Shadow Folders

There's a legend often whispered by the longtime users of Visual SourceSafe. They say
that back in the old days, before Visual SourceSafe, they had to manually duplicate their
work into more than one directory for testing. The horror! Well, over-the-top perhaps, but
all the same, the introduction of Shadow Folders gave many developers a reason to sigh in
relief. In Chapter 10, "Backing Up Projects," you learned about using Shadow Folders for
archiving your work and your Visual SourceSafe database. Well, contrary to what you may
believe, this is not the Shadow Folder's actual intended purpose.

Shadow folders were created to give you a means of centralized deployment. A Shadow
Folder is a directory (usually on a server) that contains the latest revisions made to your
project files. Shadow Folders do not contain the master copy of the file itself; instead,
each time a change is made to the file in SourceSafe, the newest version is copied to the
Shadow Folder. Your working copy remains in its working directory and your master copy
still sits safely within the SourceSafe database.

Why would you use this? Shadow Folders give you a convenient one-stop-shop place to
view your work, where it is most up-to-date, before deploying your site to its live Web
server. Imagine this scenario: You and your team are working on your Web project. Each
time one of you updates a file in the database, you manually GET the most recent version to
your test server. After a hectic day of many changes, every single member of your team
(including you) has to manually GET each of your changed files to the test server so that
you can make sure everything is up to snuff. Not a pleasant thought, having your team
spending so much time simply copying a current version after each update.

Shadow Folders are the solution to this tedium. Every time you update a project file and
check it back into the database, they spring into action by copying the latest revision to
the destination. There is no need to manually copy the current edition; it is done without
you even blinking an eye. Like a faithful toady, it duplicates your work without you breaking a sweat. And let's face it, who doesn't want a lackey?

When you are ready to make your Shadow Folder, choose Tools, Options from the Visual
SourceSafe Administrator menu bar. Choose the Shadow Folders tab from the Options
dialog box, as shown in Figure 12.13.

FIG. 12.13

Use the Shadow Folders tab to choose your project and the Shadow Folder's location. You can also change the behavior of the copies.

This simple dialog box provides you with two text boxes to set the source project and the Shadow Folder's destination. In addition to these two text boxes, there are a few options for controlling how the files' copies are to behave:

- Set Shadow Folder for Project. This is the first text box, where you specify your source project. Your project path, in the form of $/Project, is entered here. You may optionally click the Browse button to select your project using the graphical user interface.

- Set Shadow Folder To. The second text box is your destination, or your Shadow Folder. This is the directory where all of your revisions are copied. This may be either a local directory or a local area network path. You may optionally click the Browse button to use the graphical user interface to find the destination path.

- Set Read-Only Flag for Files. This sole check box lets you determine if all files copied into the Shadow Folder are read-only. If you choose to have the copies read-only, they will not be writable in this directory.

- End-of-Line Character for Files. By default, the character at the end of each line of text is a combination carriage return (CR) and line feed (LF). If, for your needs, this should be different, you can choose to change them to only carriage returns or only line feeds from the drop down list.

- File Date/Time. By default, when your latest revision is copied to the Shadow Folder, the current date and time are stamped to your file's attributes. You may choose to change this from the drop down list to be the date/time that the file was modified, or when the file was checked into the SourceSafe database.

Jose Gets into the Shadows

Each morning, it was part of Jose's routine to check over the newest changes in the Web site. He usually liked to check the site over before the developers arrived so that he would have a list of points to go over with them. Unfortunately, several of the new developers failed to get their revisions to the test server in a timely fashion. More than once Jose was forced to do the job himself, or miss the revision entirely. Frustrated by this, Jose took matters into his own hands by setting up Shadow Folders for the Web site. Now, each time a developer made a change the test server was automatically updated with the newest revision, ensuring that each time Jose looked at the site it was the most current work. If only he could get them to submit their time cards as easily.

From Here...

Having graduated from "Visual SourceSafe Administrator's College," you're ready to move on to the more frivolous topics in this book, such as:

- Chapter 13, "Integration," primes you on using Visual SourceSafe 5.0 with development environments. If you think you're too good for the SourceSafe Explorer, you're ready to move on to this ground.

- Chapter 15, "SourceSafe Utilities," completes your post-graduate work in administrative tasks. The utilities included with SourceSafe provide you the tools to carry out important tasks. Don't hide now, you're almost done.

- Appendix B, "Visual SourceSafe Options Summary," teaches you everything you wanted to know about SourceSafe's options. If you want a definition of every option available to you in both the SourceSafe Explorer and Administrator, this is your reading material for the bathroom.

Part
IV

Ch
12

CHAPTER 13

Integration

Web tools aplenty

Not surprisingly, Microsoft's own Web development tools offer direct Visual SourceSafe integration. Both Microsoft FrontPage and Visual InterDev let you control revisions to your heart's content.

It's a programmer's world

The development environments that started it all—the programmer's IDE. The people at Microsoft, shrewd as they are, offer complete SourceSafe integration in their programming environments as well. Do you detect a pattern here?

No IDE for me

Not using one of the Microsoft- or Visual SourceSafe-compatible environments? Although you are a second-class citizen, you have options other than going without Visual SourceSafe.

All work in Visual SourceSafe Explorer makes a Web developer a dull person. Visual SourceSafe is not only usable as a standard tool, but it can also be used in many *development environments*. What exactly is a development environment, you ask? Good question. Here's the answer: Development environments (often referred to as an integrated development environment, or *IDE*) were the logical evolution of dissimilar programming tools in the past. Before IDEs, programmers used many different tools to do the job. These included a *compiler* (called from a command line), an *editor* (to actually write the source code), and often a *debugger* (to test the quality of the code and pick out errors). The biggest problem with this situation is that it required a programmer to run these programs separate of one another, or write a series of scripts (called *batch files*) to complete a task. There had to be a better way. This was like running Microsoft Word to type your document, but needing to load several different programs to check spelling and to print.

Pre-Windows, several companies got an idea. What if they were to deliver a tool to programmers that not only had their beloved compiler, but also an editor (and often a debugger), all in one friendly program? No jumping between programs, no need to write batch files. All the simpler. This way of approaching the development tools became known as the integrated development environment, simply because all the important tools had been combined into one. Development environments are now the norm in programming and they are beginning to become a presence in Web development. The underlying idea is to provide developers with one software application where they can do the majority of their work. All of the Microsoft development tools provide an IDE. In fact, several Microsoft products share the same IDE, called Visual Studio. Microsoft C++, Visual J++, and Visual InterDev all use Visual Studio.

Visual SourceSafe provides a number of *hooks* into several different development environments, allowing you to use SourceSafe's features without ever having to leave your IDE. These hooks make using Visual SourceSafe easier in many environments. For example, Microsoft Visual Studio directly links with Visual SourceSafe and lets you check files in and out of the database from a single menu. For environments that do not directly have support for Visual SourceSafe, there are other options, so you're not left out of the mix. ■

Visual SourceSafe and Authoring Tools

The market for Web development and authoring tools is a growing one. Teeming hordes of designers titillated by the prospect of "getting on the Web" have fostered an industry of Web editors and third-party tools to ease the job. Authoring tools come in two basic varieties:

1. For those artists who don't know or care what a line of HTML looks like, the *What You See Is What You Get* (WYSIWYG) Web authoring tools let them work in a sheltered world. Not unlike a desktop publishing application, these tools are aimed at the designer or less technically inclined crowd to make Web design more like publishing.

2. For those who crave a challenge and like to type, the HTML editor takes you into the heart of Web development by making hand coding easier. Not entirely hiding you from the work at hand, HTML editors expand the functionality of coding from NotePad and add an array of tools.

Microsoft offers two products that address these two markets—Microsoft FrontPage and Microsoft Visual InterDev. Both of these tools have been created to appeal to two different segments of the Web developer market. To be honest, elements of FrontPage appear in Visual InterDev, so you may want to consider Visual InterDev more than a technically inclined environment. These two tools take advantage of Visual SourceSafe's integration features. That's not surprising, considering all three products come from the same happy home.

Enabling Visual SourceSafe Integration

Before you can use the integrated SourceSafe features in these programs, you must install the Visual SourceSafe components used for integration. If you did not install the SourceSafe integration components when you first installed Visual SourceSafe, you must do so now. Follow these instructions:

1. From the Add/Remove Programs control panel, select Microsoft Visual SourceSafe V5.0 and click the Add/Remove button.

2. Click the Add/Remove button to install the component. The Visual SourceSafe Setup program appears and begins to scan your system for installed components. Once the scan is complete, the Setup dialog box appears, shown in Figure 13.1.

3. From the Maintenance Mode dialog box, shown in Figure 13.2, select the Enable SourceSafe Integration option. This tells the Setup program to install the needed components into your existing installation.

FIG. 13.1

The Visual SourceSafe Setup dialog box lets you control nearly every aspect of your installation.

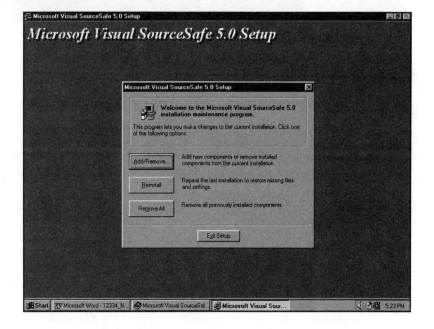

Part
IV

Ch
13

4. Click the Continue button to begin the installation. After confirming that your system has the required disk space, the Setup program dutifully copies the required files into the appropriate locations.

5. After the installation is complete, the Setup program informs you that the installation was successful. Click the OK button to close the Setup program.

Visual SourceSafe's integration features are now available to your development tools.

FIG. 13.2
The Maintenance
dialog box lets you
add and remove
components from
your installation.

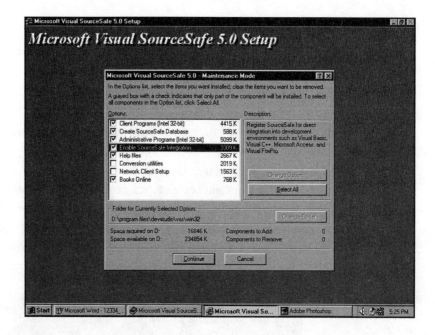

Microsoft FrontPage

Amidst the jungle of competing WYSIWYG authoring tools is Microsoft's own FrontPage,
acquired from Vermeer Technologies. FrontPage provides you with a fully WYSIWYG
authoring environment, in addition to simplified Web site management tools. Although
you can use FrontPage to create your Web sites and manually publish them, FrontPage
includes *server extensions* for Web publishing. These extensions allow you to edit your
Web sites and immediately deploy them to the Web server, without ever having to leave
FrontPage. You must have the extensions installed on your Web server to take advantage
of this feature.

Starting with Visual SourceSafe in FrontPage   Before you can begin using Visual
SourceSafe features from inside FrontPage, you must specify a source control project
name for your Web site. To do so, follow these steps:

1. Open your Web site from within the FrontPage Explorer.

2. Choose Tools, Web Settings from the menu bar. The FrontPage Web Settings dialog
   box appears.

3. Select the Configuration tab, as shown in Figure 13.3.

4. The third text box, Source Control Project, lets you specify your project name.
   Enter the Visual SourceSafe path for your project. This should be in the format of
   `$/Project`.

FIG. 13.3

The FrontPage Web Settings dialog lets you specify options for your FrontPage Web.

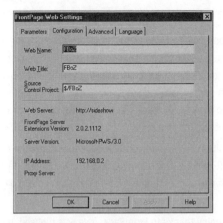

5. Click OK to commit your changes and close the dialog box.

Checking Your Files In and Out Working with the SourceSafe facilities is simplified within Microsoft FrontPage. The process of obtaining a file from the VSS database is automatic, once you check out a file your most recent version is retrieved from the database and placed into your working directory. From there, whenever you make a modification to a file and check your work back into the SourceSafe database, Front-Page does the legwork and lets you snooze on the job. To check out a file, follow these two steps:

1. Select your file from the file list within the FrontPage Explorer.
2. From the menu bar, choose Edit, Check Out. This carries out the task of getting your most recent version and checking the file out of the database.

Once you are done modifying your file, you are ready to fire it back up to the database and lay it to rest. To check in your file, follow these two steps:

1. Select your file from the file list within the FrontPage Explorer.
2. Choose Edit, Check In from the menu bar. Your working copy is checked into the database and your local copy is removed from your working directory.

If you have decided not to modify your document after you have checked it out, you can undo your checkout by following these two steps:

1. From the FrontPage Explorer, select your file in the file list.
2. Choose Edit, Undo Check Out. This removes your file's local working copy and cancels the check out from the SourceSafe database. Your file is available for check out once again.

Part
IV

Ch
13

Jose Loves FrontPage

Jose always felt somewhat left out, creatively. He was a project manager, a cog in the wheel. When it came time to update the Site Corporati intranet, Jose had his chance to contribute. Marge and the Web development crew were preoccupied with the finishing touches for the Fliedermaus Bank of Zurich Web project, meaning that they couldn't contribute to the work that needed to be done. Picking up a copy of Microsoft FrontPage, Jose saw his chance to play with Web authoring and create something magical.

Using Visual SourceSafe to organize and manage his site, Jose found that the convenient integration features made his life simpler. Not being used to this Web thing, he often made mistakes that killed the functionality of the intranet. With SourceSafe he could quickly roll back to a previous version.

With the intranet site up and running thanks to FrontPage, Jose was pleased. It may not win any awards for beauty (according to Marge), but it did the job. "Who knows," thought Jose, "maybe there's a career in Web design for me after all..."

Microsoft Visual InterDev

Microsoft FrontPage is targeted for Web designers and publishers who would rather not deal with the intricacies of HTML. Visual InterDev is targeted for advanced Web developers who not only want to work with HTML, but also want to work with the next generation of Web publishing tools. Direct integration of database support, ActiveX controls, Active Server Pages, and Active Layout make Visual InterDev a powerful tool. With Visual InterDev it is possible to develop complete Web applications without ever leaving the program, thanks in part to its support for FrontPage server extensions. In addition to the server extensions, Visual InterDev includes a specialized version of the FrontPage WYSIWYG editor for those who do not want to author pages in raw HTML alone. The main difference in the Visual InterDev edition of FrontPage is that it uses the Visual InterDev tools for Web management, as opposed to the FrontPage Explorer in the regular package.

Starting with Visual SourceSafe in Visual InterDev   You will find that working with Visual SourceSafe in Visual InterDev is simpler than the standard SourceSafe Explorer. To begin working with SourceSafe, you must first enable source control within your Visual InterDev project:

1. With your Visual InterDev project open, choose Project, Web Project, Enable Source Control from the menu bar.

2. The Enable Source Control dialog box appears as shown in Figure 13.4, asking you to enter a name for your project in Visual SourceSafe. Enter the project name using a standard SourceSafe path, such as $/Project.

FIG. 13.4

When you enable source control for your Visual InterDev project, you are prompted for a project name, which will be used for your Web site within Visual SourceSafe.

3. Click OK to start the process.

4. Dependent on your project's size, the addition of your files to Visual SourceSafe may take some time. Once the process is complete, a confirmation dialog box appears to confirm that you have successfully added your Web project to source control. Click OK to close the dialog box.

Checking Your Files In and Out   Every time you add a file to your Visual InterDev Web project, you are also automatically adding it to the Visual SourceSafe database. With the addition step removed, you only deal with checking files in and out of the database for editing. Visual SourceSafe automatically sets the working directory for your Web project to the directory where you created your project. Each time you are about to edit a file, Visual InterDev requests the master copy from the Visual SourceSafe database. To check out a file, follow these two steps:

1. From the project file view, select the file you are going to modify.

2. To check out the file you may either double-click it, or right-click and choose Get Working Copy from the menu. This retrieves the working copy from the database and places it in your working directory. You can then edit the file in a window.

With the file checked out, the icon to the left of the file name changes to a color icon. This is a quick way of telling that you have a file checked out and in your working directory.

After you have completed your modifications to the file, you are ready to check the file back into the database. To check in your changes, follow these two steps:

1. Again from the project file view, select the file you need to check in.

2. Right-click the file and choose Release Working Copy from the menu. This updates the database with your changes and updates your file on your Web server.

Now that you have checked in your file, the icon to the left of the file name returns to a grayed-out version of itself. This is Visual InterDev's standard method for identifying files that are not present in the working directory.

Part

IV

Ch

13

Marge Gets Visual (InterDev)

To save on some of the development work for the programmers, elements of the FBoZ Web project were moved to Microsoft's Internet Information Server 3.0 and Active Server Pages. Using Active Server Pages, Marge could develop server-side interactivity into the Web site without requiring the assistance of a programmer. To simplify the job, Marge began to work with Microsoft Visual InterDev. Using Visual InterDev's SourceSafe integration to keep her work secure and sound, Marge began to play with the active scripting in the Web site. By using Visual InterDev, Marge accomplished something she'd wanted for a long time: shunning Jeff.

Visual SourceSafe and Development Tools

Nearly all of Microsoft's programming tools share the same development environment—the Developer Studio. In fact, Visual InterDev also uses the Developer Studio interface, but the Visual SourceSafe integration within InterDev behaves differently. Microsoft Visual C++, Visual J++, and Visual Studio use the Developer Studio interface. Only Microsoft Visual Basic and Visual FoxPro use a different interface while still supporting Visual SourceSafe integration. In addition to Microsoft products, development environments from other vendors support revision control systems. Using Visual SourceSafe in these environments is beyond the scope of this book. You should refer to the documentation included with each package for information specific to Visual SourceSafe.

Jeff and Visual C++

Jeff spends the majority of his time in Microsoft Visual C++. That being his preferred development environment, he has customized his Developer Studio interface to work efficiently for him. With the SourceSafe integration features present in Developer Studio, Jeff could still easily manage and control his source code development without ever having to leave Visual C++.

On more than one occasion while developing a new CGI, Jeff encountered problems with his code. He needed to roll back to a previous version several times. Thanks to SourceSafe and Developer Studio, he could do so without breaking a sweat and wasting time switching programs. Jeff was so pleased, he made a mental note to treat himself to a self-indulgent insult at Marge's expense.

Integration Using Command Line Tools

For some authoring tools, there simply is no option of integration with a revision control system and Visual SourceSafe. Thankfully, there is another option. Many authoring tools support external applications (a fallback from the old pre-IDE days). If your application supports calling external applications or batch files, often using macros, you have the ability to create intricate batch files using the Visual SourceSafe Command Line tools. These tools offer complete SourceSafe functionality without a graphical user interface. For information on creating batch files and using the Command Line tools, please refer to Chapter 14, "Command Line Tools."

From Here...

You're in the home stretch of this book: time to get up on your feet and sprint to the finish line. Elements upcoming in the book:

- Chapter 14, "Command Line Tools," spouts the virtues of the Visual SourceSafe Command Line Tools. Not content to work in a GUI? Itching for some batch files? This is the chapter that will give you that command line fix.

- Chapter 15, "SourceSafe Utilities," continues on the Command Line thread by exploring the utilities included with your Visual SourceSafe distribution. This is your chance to dig deeper into the depths of SourceSafe and the Command Line.

- Chapter 16, "Cross-Platform Usage," ends the book's chapters on a high note: homogenous computing. If you are working in an environment that is filled with more than just PCs running Microsoft Windows, you may want to learn all that you can about Visual SourceSafe on other platforms. This is just for you Apple Macintosh and UNIX people.

Part
IV

Ch
13

CHAPTER 14

Command Line Tools

Sometimes you have to go backward in order to go forward. The thought of a dreaded command line sends many neophyte users into trembling shock. You don't have to fear Visual SourceSafe's command line interface in order to use it, though. There are many reasons to use a command line processor, especially in VSS. ■

Back when people typed...

Learn how your ancestors entered commands in the old days—by typing them. You can also find out why you would want to do it now.

Offline processing

Learn how to tweak command line technology to magically make things happen, even when you're not there.

The Visual SourceSafe Command Line

For those of you who weren't born before World War II, you should know what a command line is. It's an interface based on typed commands instead of the quick and easy point-and-click. It's also a very powerful and flexible interface, capable of producing results faster and more efficiently than most graphical user interface systems. This is because a command line doesn't have to deal with the overhead of maintaining a menu system, graphic displays, and other computer-intensive bells and whistles. Unfortunately, a command line is one of the most arcane user interfaces you can have. If you don't speak its language, you don't get anywhere. At least you can randomly point and click around in a GUI.

If you're feeling guilty about forcing the programmers of Visual SourceSafe to make a command line system just so you don't use it, don't. The existing command line interface is actually a throwback to SourceSafe 3.0 (note the lack of "Visual"). Because there has been no change to the implementation, you should feel right at home if you are an experienced SourceSafe 3.0 veteran. If you aren't, then roll up your sleeves and get ready to learn.

Setting the Command Line Options

Before you can do any hacking, you should set the options for your command line experience in the Visual SourceSafe Explorer. From here you can set constraints on your commenting style and working folder preferences. To set your command line options you must:

1. Choose Tools, Options.
2. Click the Command Line Options tab (you may have to scroll to the left to see it).
3. Set your options as you desire.
4. Click OK to save your changes.

The first two options from the dialog box in Figure 14.1 deal with how the command line system interacts with your working folder. In the Visual SourceSafe Explorer, you could navigate between projects simply by clicking, but would set your working directory on a one-time basis. In the command line system your current directory is your working directory, which reverses the priority established in the Explorer. In the command line it's the current project you have to set through a declaration, and the working directory is declared simply by navigating through your directory structure. However, you can still set a working directory, either from the command line or those you've already defined in the Visual SourceSafe Explorer.

FIG. 14.1

A configured command line is a happy command line.

The first check box, Assume Working Folder Based on Current Project, determines which working folder to use, the current directory, or the predefined working folder for that project. When checked, this option forces SourceSafe to use whatever working folder is currently associated with that project. When left blank, SourceSafe puts working files into the current directory, which it assumes is the working folder.

The second check box, Assume Project Based on Working Folder, is an inverse function to Assume Working Folder Based on Current Project. SourceSafe checks what directory you are currently in when you execute a command line procedure. If the current directory is the working folder for one of your projects and you have this option checked, then SourceSafe will point to that project when executing your command. If it is not checked, the command will be carried out as usual.

The next block of options demonstrated in Figure 14.1 deals with Check Out Comments and how they're processed in the command line. You may only select one of the three options. The first is the simplest: No Comment on Check Out. This means all check out operations occur without being commented. No fuss, no mess, no worry. The second option is Apply Same Comment to All Files; that only makes you enter one comment, which is then applied to all of the files. The last option is Apply Different Comment to Each File, which makes you apply a different comment to each check out action.

The Check Out Comment options deal with how many comments you have to enter. The Comment Prompt options deal with how you enter those comments. The first option, Prompt for Comments on the Command Line, will demand a comment from the command line interface as you are executing the check out. The Use Editor to Prompt for Comments option will call up your text/code editor to make the comment. The Use Prompt String check box will place an "insert comment here" string into your editor when it opens a file to be commented. The Editor area allows you to browse to your editing software for adding comments.

Using the Command Line

The difference between command line and graphical-based interfaces is one of memory. In a command line situation you have to memorize several key words and their use if you want to get anything done. In a graphical situation you can look at little icons that trigger a visual memory, or navigate through a hierarchical menu system that is grouped by topic. If you find yourself getting confused on the command line, just try plugging in the Visual SourceSafe commands you can remember from the Explorer. The concepts behind check in, check out, and get are the same as they always were. The new confusion lies in getting around the project system, and the fact that in the command line interface everything is one word instead of two.

One of the most confusing things about the Visual SourceSafe command line interface is the fact that it doesn't replace your command prompt. You run the SourceSafe executable (SS.EXE) with a variety of command line options following it. Think of it as similar to a DOS command, but in this case SS has to preface every command you enter. When commands are referred to in this chapter's following sections it's assumed that SS will come before them, as displayed in the examples. Some text in the following examples is italicized. Italicized text should not be entered verbatim, but replaced with the appropriate command, username, password, and so on.

> **NOTE** All of the procedures following have to take place from a command prompt. In Windows 95 parlance this means you either have to open an MS-DOS prompt or type a command into the Run menu. For multiple and complex commands, you should use the DOS prompt, as it's more convenient than having to go to <u>R</u>un from your Start menu all the time. ■

Navigating Through Projects and Working Folders   Visual SourceSafe is based on security—hence the name "safe." In the command line you can't just log in like you can in a graphical user interface. Every command that either allows information out of the VSS database, or may change information in it, must be verified with a user account. There are two ways you can log onto the command line in Visual SourceSafe. The first is to simply type your command as you normally would, without any user information. Before proceeding, Visual SourceSafe will ask for your name and password. The second method is to add the -Y command line option to the end of your SourceSafe command:

```
SS <some command> -YJose,J0sePASS
```

The first thing after the -Y is the user's account name. If a password is required to access that account you have to include it after a comma, as in the previous example. There is no space between the comma and the text, nor is there space between the -Y and the user name. A good mnemonic for this is to think "Yuser information."

Way back in Chapter 1, "Visual SourceSafe Concepts," you learned that Visual SourceSafe works just like your operating system when it comes to organizing files. If you remember this fact, you should have no problem adapting to command line navigation. If your hard

drive's root directory is C:\, then your Visual SourceSafe database root project is $/.
You can navigate between projects using a command similar to MS-DOS's CD, which in
Visual SourceSafe vernacular becomes CP (change project). The DOS functionality is
carried throughout, so you can "CP .." to go up one project level, or "CP $/Bank of
Zurich/Web" to change to an exact address. Just remember that the front slash (/)
replaces the back slash (\) when it comes to denoting projects. To change to the root
project without having to log in, type

```
SS CP $/ -YUsername,Password
```

The biggest problem here is that you are going through the SS.EXE program and not a
shell, like you normally do in DOS mode. Hence, you have no feedback as to location:
In what project are you? Where is it in the hierarchical chain? Fortunately, you can determine at what project Visual SourceSafe is currently pointing using the project command.
Keep in mind, though, that each user is probably looking at a different project at any one
time. It's important to make sure you have the correct user account to access the right
areas. To get an idea of what project you're currently working in, type

```
SS project -YUsername,Password
```

Searching Through Projects the Command Line Way   Knowing what project you are in
is all well and good, but it's not very effective if you don't know what other projects make
up the tree. Use the directory command to get a breakdown of the database's project
structure. Once again, this will vary from user to user, depending on the current project,
so make sure you get your -Y information right. To display a directory you must type

```
SS directory -YUsername,Password
```

A directory is great, but what about when you need a specific file? It's not as if you can
pull down the Search menu like you can in the VSS Explorer. What you need is a seek
and destroy type of command. Luckily for you, the good people who programmed Visual
SourceSafe included the Locate command. In order to make sure you actually have access
to a file, Visual SourceSafe won't locate a file without your user information. To locate a
particular file you must type

```
SS locate Default.ASP -YUsername,Password
```

Lastly comes the all-important assignment of the working folder. The working folder is a
bit more important in the command line setting. It's easy to get confused as to what directory you're actually working in, and what project you're currently on. If you already have a
logical and concise working folder arrangement, you might want to keep it. The working
folder command has two main arguments. The first is the project to which you are assigning a working folder. The second is the working directory itself. To set a working folder
for a project you must type

```
SS Workfold $/Bank of Zurich C:\Temp -YUsername,Password
```

Remember to start the reference to the project with $/, and to use traditional C:\DOS nomenclature when referring to your working folder.

General Library Services

You can do everything that you want inside the command line interface that you could inside the Visual SourceSafe Explorer. Once again, though, the problem is keeping track of what is checked out and what is just hanging around in the working folder. Remember to append your user identification to commands, so you don't have to fiddle with dialogs.

N O T E   There are many more commands and further options modifying them. This chapter is meant more to familiarize you with the general procedures to the command line interface than a complete breakdown of VSS's command line. ■

▶ **See** Appendix A, "Batch Files and Command Line Options," on **p. 215** for a specific summary of all command line options.

Once again you learn another way to check out files. The thing to remember here is that the command is checkout and not "check out." To check out a file you must first make sure you've navigated to its project, or that you know its exact project address. If the file you want to check out is in your current project, you only have to supply the file's name. If the file is outside of your current project, you need its full address. To check out a file you must type

```
SS checkout $/Bank of Zurich/Web/Default.ASP -YUsername,Password
```

Obviously, if you have the ability to check out a file you must also be able to check it back in. Once again, the command line interpreter wants checkin and not "check in." You can check in a file from anywhere in the directory structure, and Visual SourceSafe will remember where it came from, so you don't have to specify a return project. To check in a file you must type

```
SS checkin Default.ASP -YUsername,Password
```

You have to be careful again when adding files. Make sure that you have the right project selected before you go around adding files to it. Don't be afraid to make liberal use of the project and CP commands to find out where you are, and to move where you want to go. To manipulate long file names with any of the file-based commands you must enclose the file name in quotes, just as you do in the MS-DOS prompt. To add a file to the current project you must type

```
SS add Default.ASP Index.HTM "Bank of Zurich Special File.HTM"
➥-YUsername,Password
```

You need to create a project before you can go rustling files to add to a project. When creating projects in the command line environment you have two options for addressing the new project. If you want it to be a subfolder of your current project, just type in the name. If you want to create a project outside of your current project, you have to enter the exact address from the root ($/). To create a project you have to type

```
SS Create $/Bank of Zurich/Web/Graphics -YUsername,Password
```

It's publish or perish, and the Get command is your only ally in this dog-eat-dog world. Get is just as flexible in the command line setting as it is in the graphical Explorer. You can publish to any path that follows the Universal Naming Convention (UNC), and you don't necessarily have to use a drive letter. To get a file you must type

```
SS get $/Bank of Zurich/Web/Default.ASP \\Marge\testing\123
➥-YUsername,Password
```

Lastly comes the chaotic act of destruction—deleting. As you may know, Visual SourceSafe has two deletion states. The first is a simple delete, which removes the file's name from a project listing, but doesn't erase the file itself from the database. This file can be recovered. The second option is to destroy a file, which irrevocably removes it from the VSS database. The syntax for both commands is identical, but make sure you don't get them mixed up! Both act upon a file in the current project. In order to act upon other projects you have to navigate to them. To delete or destroy, enter the following:

```
SS delete Default.ASP -YUsername,Password
SS destroy Default.ASP -YUsername,Password
```

Of course, you might have been too hasty with that there delete command. It's a strangely human impulse to erroneously delete material, and this aspect of our nature has cost the world billions of dollars. Fortunately, if you've only deleted the file, you can just as easily recover it. Destroy, however, is the file equivalent of being hit by an atom-smasher, so there's no hope for you there. To undelete or recover a file you must type

```
SS recover Default.ASP -YUser,Password
```

That's a lot of memorizing to do, isn't it? Now you see why many people prefer a GUI over the more powerful (yet clumsier) command line. If you are totally stumped about commands, don't worry. You can define your own command line parameters that mirror or combine the standard Visual SourceSafe options.

Alternate Commands

Not everyone is used to SourceSafe's command set, or maybe you're just feeling perverse. Either way, you can assign your own name to your favorite Visual SourceSafe command line parameters. Do you think checkin should be "fuzzybunny" instead? Go ahead! Nobody but you and your Administrator will know. Another common reason to assign

Part
IV

Ch
14

multiple definitions to a SourceSafe command is to grant compatibility with other Revision Control Systems. If you're used to the UNIX RCS system, you can modify the command text to something with which you're familiar.

Fittingly, to define alternate commands you need to get your hands dirty and edit the SS.INI file. The SS.INI controls what options specifically apply to you. Every user in your Visual SourceSafe system has a unique SS.INI just for them. By default, the SS.INI is stored in your user directory. A common place to look for it would then be C:\VSS\USERS\ JOSE, (replace JOSE with whatever your name may be). Any simple text editor will work fine on the .INI file. If this is the first time you've added commands to it, there won't be a predefined "command" space in the SS.INI. Following is an example of what you could put in your SS.INI. Remember that the SS.INI file operates on a user-by-user level, so these commands will be unique to your account.

N O T E The syntax for defining new commands is *New Command = Standard Visual SourceSafe command.* Your new command must be one word in length. The new command is whatever alternate you will be using, and the Standard command is whatever function you'll be duplicating. Assigning an alternate command wording to a standard one in no way affects the function of the original.

> *New Command = Standard Visual SourceSafe command*
>
> *Borrow = checkout*
>
> *Nuke = destroy*

```
[Commands]
fuzzybunny = checkout
chicken = checkin
IHateJeff = get
```

The Visual SourceSafe command line already has some alternate commands hardwired into the program itself in order to ease the transition time for UNIX users. They are listed in Table 14.1.

Table 14.1 Predefined Alternate Commands in Visual SourceSafe

Alternate Command	VSS Standard Command
CD	CP
ChPro	CP
Copy	Share and Branch
Remove	Delete
Grep	Find

Alternate Command	VSS Standard Command
LS	Directory
MD	Create
MkPro	Create
MP	Create
Type	View
Undelete	Recover
WhereIs	Locate
Scan	FindInFiles
Separate	Branch
Uncheckout	UndoCheckout
Update	CheckIn

Creating Batch Files

Most of you probably look upon the command line as a historical oddity, included in the VSS package more as a museum piece than anything else. However, there's more to command line operations than just a lot of typing.

You are capable of *batch processing* using the command line interpreter. The main idea behind this is that you don't have to be shackled to your desk performing repetitious tasks that require a "Press any key to continue" every ten seconds and nothing else. The main problem with most graphical user interfaces is the fact that you have to be in charge at all times. You can't just say "All right VSS, you check in all 3,000 of those files; I'm going out for some coffee." If you could do that, the people who depend on the arcane nature of computers (technical book publishers, for example) would be out of business. However, with the command line you can come close to that dream, as long as you put some work into it up front.

Visual SourceSafe accepts instructions at the command prompt, but it will also take them from a file that contains commands. In MS-DOS dialect this is known as a *batch file*, as it is a batch of commands following one another. When you have created a batch file properly, it can run at any time without intervention from anyone. An obvious use for them would be maintenance or those huge check in/check out operations that leave your clicking finger numb. The most important attribute of a batch operation is the fact that you can leave them to run unsupervised and still pretend to be working.

Part

IV

Ch

14

To create a batch file all you need is a simple text editor and at least a basic understanding of the command line processes. Literally all you will be doing is typing one command after another. The skill in creating batch files is realizing where you can save yourself time and effort by doing things in the command line, or in the Explorer. Maintenance is another aspect to consider. There are several third-party utilities that can execute a file at a certain time, which could help keep your VSS database clean and healthy. For example, if you wanted to update content on a regular basis you could have a batch file that would Get all of the relevant files every midnight. Both Windows NT and Windows 95 come with scheduling functionality—it all depends on what you want to do.

Command line processes can use wild cards, which can make your batch files that much friendlier when it comes to naming every single file in a certain project. Following is an example batch file to Get all files in the $/Bank of Zurich/Web project:

```
REM Batch file to publish all web files to local server for testing
REM Created 97/06/22 by Marge
CD \\Marge\Testing\123
SS get "$/Bank of Zurich/Web" -R -I- -YMarge,E0las
REM The project address with spaces has to be enclosed in quotes, much like
➥a long file REM name.
```

You can Get an entire project if you refer to it by the project name instead of a series of file names. The -R flag is the recursive flag, which will include all of the selected project's subfolders. The -I- flag is the most important one to remember in batch processing, as it tells Visual SourceSafe to ignore any input requests from that object. It's this flag that allows batch processes to run uninterrupted. Note that long file names, or file names with spaces, have to appear in quotes. However, be sure to begin and end the quote at the right time. Don't include the flags and options themselves in the quotation. When you are Getting these files, Visual SourceSafe will assume your current directory is the working folder, and the destination of your files. That's why the first command in the batch is a DOS command, to change directories.

NOTE In order for batch files to work outside of your Visual SourceSafe executable directory, you need to have the SS.EXE available through your path statement. Otherwise, you simply get "bad command or file name" as your operating system looks for an executable that it can't find. Consult your operating system documentation for information on defining your PATH statement in DOS. ∎

The reasons to use batch files are many: convenience, speed, and unmonitored activity. While the actual process of creating them is a bit more arcane than just check in/check out, the effort is worth it if it saves you time in the long run. However, there is a caveat attached to any batch process: Because they can run uninterrupted, batch files can also be a dangerous tool in the hands of the malicious or foolish. It's just as easy to create a batch file to destroy all of your files as it is to check them out. Once again, security is paramount. A malicious user can't access Visual SourceSafe functions through the command line unless he or she has a user account in that database. If the user can't fill out the -Y information, then he or she can't actually do anything in your system. Always guard your account data carefully—especially passwords. Everyone has heard the story of the careless administrator who got his vital passwords tattooed on his forearm. Don't repeat that mistake.

From Here...

You've learned all about Visual SourceSafe's command line and what it can do for you. What remains for you to think about is how you can adapt your operations to use the advantages the command line grants. If you are engaging in repetitious work that could easily be executed unmonitored by a batch file, make one. You can claim to be doing the same amount of work, but this way you'll have more time to goof off. To supplement your learning you should investigate:

Chapter 15, "SourceSafe Utilities." This chapter contains a breakdown on all of the included utilities that come with your Visual SourceSafe package. Many of these can be helpful when dealing with command line situations.

Appendix A, "Batch Files and Command Line Options." This appendix is a complete list of every command line and option that could fit into the book. Use this as a reference when creating your own batch files.

Part
IV

Ch
14

SourceSafe Utilities

Visual SourceSafe cannot be all things to all people. As for many applications, you may need additional programs to address problems introduced by Visual SourceSafe. Both Microsoft and third-party vendors offer those additional programs. ■

Something for nothing

Nearly a dozen separate utilities are included with Visual SourceSafe. Each of these utilities fulfills a certain need. If you're feeling needy, start here.

Everything not Microsoft

Microsoft does not hold an exclusive license to add-on utilities. Several third parties offer solutions to SourceSafe problems.

Included Utilities

Visual SourceSafe includes several utilities with the distribution media. You may use these utilities to solve several problems faced by users moving to Visual SourceSafe. If you are moving from an existing revision control system and are looking to convert your existing database to SourceSafe, Microsoft has provided a few tools for doing just that. Additionally, they have provided several general administrative tools that you may find of importance to your installation.

These utilities are located in the WIN32 subdirectory of your Visual SourceSafe installation directory. You may want to add the WIN32 directory to your system's path to avoid entering the directory path to the command each time. Comprehensive information on each of these utilities is included in the Visual SourceSafe Books Online. If you find yourself asking questions that you don't find an answer for here, refer to the Books Online.

ANALYZE.EXE

The `Analyze` command line utility gives you a tool to analyze your SourceSafe database if you suspect its data integrity. In addition to analyzing, you may use this tool to repair databases that have "fallen ill" to errors. Possible errors include checksum failures due to file corruption or hard drive problems. Microsoft recommends that you run this utility at least once a month, perhaps more, to verify that you have no problems with your Visual SourceSafe database. Carrying out an analysis on your database is usually a simple process. As with any administrative task involving the database, you should have all of your users log out before proceeding. To begin, follow these steps:

1. Using the Visual SourceSafe Administrator, lock your database to prevent users from accessing it during the analysis. Refer to Chapter 12, "Visual SourceSafe Administration," for information on locking your database.

2. From a command prompt, run the `Analyze` command. If you do not have your Visual SourceSafe WIN32 folder in your path, you need to specify it in the command line. To run the `Analyze` command, type the following line and strike the Enter key:

   ```
   <SourceSafe WIN32 directory path>\Analyze <SourceSafe DATA
   ➥directory path>
   ```

3. You will see any problems the `Analyze` program encounters in a results window. If you encounter problems, you should rename the BACKUP directory. If you did not encounter any problems, your database is in fine shape and you are done.

4. With your BACKUP directory renamed, run the `Analyze` program once again, this time with a second option (remembering to hit Enter at the end of the line):

   ```
   <SourceSafe WIN32 directory path>\Analyze -f <SourceSafe
   ➥DATA directory path>
   ```

The `Analyze` program will attempt to fix the errors it has encountered when you first ran the tool.

5. Rename your BACKUP directory once again once the second run of the `Analyze` tool is complete.

6. Run `Analyze` for the third time, now with a different option. If any errors could not be fixed during the second run, they are reported during the third run. To run the `Analyze` command the third time, enter this line, followed by hitting Enter:

```
<SourceSafe WIN32 directory path>\Analyze -v4 <SourceSafe
➥DATA directory path>
```

If you find that this run has not corrected the errors, you should consult the Microsoft Knowledge Base for more information. You may also contact Microsoft Product Support Services for assistance.

N O T E The Microsoft Knowledge Base on the World Wide Web is located at **http://www. microsoft.com/kb**. This resource is invaluable if you encounter any problems using Microsoft software. For information on the Analyze tool and problems with Visual SourceSafe databases, search the Knowledge Base for article Q152807 for suggestions. ■

Your results from the `Analyze` program report to a file called ANALYZE.LOG. This file, located in a directory named BACKUP inside your DATA folder, replaces the old log each time you run the program. If `Analyze` finds corrupted files, it lists them for you in a file called ANALYZE.BAD (also placed in the BACKUP folder). When a file is repaired, the original file is placed in the BACKUP directory.

Output from `Analyze` appears in a separate window, titled Analyze Results. Before running `Analyze` again, make sure you close any open results windows. The project security is enabled when the RIGHTS.DAT file is rebuilt for your database, regardless of whether it was on or off before. Because of this change, only the Administrator will be able to log into the SourceSafe database after running the `Analyze` utility. To correct this, you should open the Visual SourceSafe Administrator to turn off project security (or reassign your users' rights).

The Analyze tool also offers extended command line options that should only be used if you are familiar with the tool. For more information on the `Analyze` tool, refer to the Microsoft Books Online.

DDCONV.EXE

When you are upgrading from an older version of Microsoft Visual SourceSafe, your database must be "brought up to muster" for the new version. The `DDConv` utility updates your old SourceSafe database into a suitable format for the new version. DDConv runs automatically at the end of each new Visual SourceSafe installation that creates a database. You may choose to run the program manually to upgrade a new, blank database using Mkss; or to rebuild some files in the database.

To upgrade an existing database, follow these steps:

1. Open a command line prompt. If you do not have the SourceSafe WIN32 folder in your path, change to that directory.

2. Enter the following line, followed by striking the Enter key:

    ```
    DDConv <path to SourceSafe DATA directory>
    ```

DDConv assumes that the SRCSAFE.INI configuration file is located in the data directory by default. If your configuration file is located elsewhere, you must specify its location by using the -m<path to SRCSAFE.INI> option. For more information on the DDConv program, refer to the Visual SourceSafe Online Books.

DELTA_SS.EXE

Microsoft Delta, the predecessor to Visual SourceSafe, is still in use by a great many development teams. If you are currently using Delta and want to convert your projects for use in Visual SourceSafe, you can easily convert them using this utility. Delta_SS extracts your files from Delta libraries and converts them to the native SourceSafe format for your database. You may choose to convert your Delta project or individual files from your project.

To convert a Delta file to Visual SourceSafe, follow these steps:

1. Open a command line prompt.

2. Type the following command, followed by hitting the Enter key:

    ```
    Delta_SS -v -r -d <path to Delta> -p <Project Name> -s
    ➡<path to VSS> -u <VSS Password> <File Name>
    ```

Once you convert your files, you can find them in a SourceSafe project with the same name your Delta project has. Your original Delta files are untouched during this process. You can find comprehensive information on using this utility in the SourceSafe Books Online.

MKSS.EXE

In Chapter 11, "Using Multiple Databases," you learned how to create additional Visual SourceSafe databases. To be completely honest, that chapter hid you from the full truth of how SourceSafe itself creates databases. When the SourceSafe Setup program goes to create a database, it in fact uses a command line utility called Mkss to create an empty database. This database is in an old Visual SourceSafe format and is not usable with the current tools. Once Mkss finishes, the Setup program runs the DDConv utility, which refurbishes your database. When that is complete—voilà—you have a fresh database.

You can use this utility to create new or alternative Visual SourceSafe databases without going through the process of running the Setup program. The process itself is very simple:

1. Open a command line prompt.

2. Enter the following line, followed by hitting Enter:

   ```
   Mkss <path to new database>
   ```

3. Run the DDConv utility to update the database to the current SourceSafe format.

PVC_SS.EXE

PVCS is one of several other revision control systems available on the market. If you are coming from a programming background, you may be very familiar with PVCS, as it is included with several development environments. Like Delta_ss, PVCS_ss has the ability to convert your entire project or individual files into a format usable by Visual SourceSafe. SourceSafe and PVCS use considerably different methods for storing data. You should be at least somewhat familiar with the Visual SourceSafe DATA directory and its structure. PVCS utilizes a different method; it uses a series of logfiles that are stored in different directory locations to track changes. Manually extracting the information from these logfiles would be prohibitive time-wise and prone to error. Thankfully, Microsoft included the PVCS_ss utility to automate the process. Unfortunately, you will not be able to transfer any labels you created in PVCS to Visual SourceSafe, as they each use a different proprietary format to store label information.

Before proceeding, you should completely back up both your PVCS project files and your SourceSafe database. Make sure that the Visual SourceSafe and PVCS executable directories are in your path. You also need to set two environment variables to identify yourself as the SourceSafe Administrator. The easiest way to do this is to set the SSUSER and SSPWD environment variables from a command prompt. Your variables should be set to:

```
Set SSUSER = ADMIN
Set SSPWD = <Your SourceSafe Administrator's Password>
```

In addition to the SSUSER and SSPWD variables, you must set four other environment variables. These should be set from your AUTOEXEC.BAT file (if you are running

Windows 95), or from the System Control Panel (if you are running Windows NT). These are the variables that you need to set:

```
set libpath = <path to the PVCS DLLs used by the GET program>
set vcsid = <userid>
set vcscfg = <path to configuration file>
set intrsolvdir = <path to the directory containing the license admin
➥facility>
```

Follow these steps to begin your conversions:

1. From a command prompt, change to the directory that contains your PVCS logfiles. These files have an extension terminated with a v.

2. Enter the following line, followed by hitting Enter:

   ```
   PVC_SS <PVCS Logfiles> <Visual SourceSafe Project>
   ```

   You may specify more than one PVCS logfile from the command line by separating them with a space. You also may optionally specify all PVCS logfiles by entering:

   ```
   PVCS_SS *.* <Visual SourceSafe Project>
   ```

   Doing this may take considerable time. Do not panic if the conversion seems to have frozen.

3. Repeat the process for any additional logfiles that you must convert.

The PVCS_SS utility is a powerful tool for your conversions. You can find comprehensive information on using this utility in the SourceSafe Books Online.

SSARC.EXE and SSRESTOR.EXE

The SSARC utility, combined with the SSRESTOR utility, provides you with a means of archiving projects and files from your SourceSafe database and restoring when required. You can also use this tool to move files and projects among databases when the need arises. SSARC creates a compressed .ZIP file containing your project files and then removes the same files from the SourceSafe database. SSRESTOR works the process in reverse by restoring your project files from the compressed ZIP archive and places them back into the database for use.

Before archiving your project files, determine what version of the files you want to archive. The SSARC utility uses the standard SourceSafe format for specifying versions (by number, date, or label). By specifying a version you can archive select versions of your work, rather than all versions in the database. When you do specify a version, SSARC archives everything up to and including that version. This simply means that if you are archiving version 5, versions 1, 2, 3, 4, and 5 are archived.

Part **IV**

Ch **15**

To archive your project files, follow these steps:

1. Open a command prompt. If you do not have the SourceSafe WIN32 directory in your path, change directories to it.

2. Insert the following command line, followed by hitting the Enter key:

   ```
   SSARC -v <Version Number> -s <Path to SRCSAFE.INI> -y
   ➡<Username,Password> <Name of Archive to Create>
   ➡<Files/Projects to Archive>
   ```

   You may specify one or more files/projects to archive. Wild cards are also acceptable. Archives are always acted on recursively.

3. Repeat the process for any additional files or projects you want to archive. Archives cannot append to existing archives, only replace or fail trying.

By default, the SSARC utility prompts you for permission before deleting the project files from the database after archiving. You can force a delete to occur by adding a -d to the command line. If you want to forbid the deletion of project files, add a -d- to the command line.

Now that you have archived your project files, you may find the need to restore them from their slumber and put them back into the database. To do so:

1. Open a command prompt. If you do not have the SourceSafe WIN32 directory in your path, change directories.

2. Insert the following command line, followed by hitting the Enter key:

   ```
   SSRESTOR -y <Username,Password> <Path to Archive to Restore>
   ➡<Files/Projects to Restore>
   ```

   If you do not specify a list of projects or files to restore, SSRESTOR will default to restoring all project files in the archive.

3. Repeat the process for any additional archives you want to restore.

SSRESTOR defaults to restoring your project files to the same SourceSafe path from which they were archived. If you want to specify a different path, you can add the -p<Project Name> option to the command line. This will place the restored project files recursively under this project.

Both the SSARC and SSRESTOR tools offer considerably more options to customize your archival and restoration tasks. For more information on these tools, refer to the Visual SourceSafe Books Online.

SSLOGIN.EXE

When you are working with a development environment that needs integration scripts, you will likely need to know the SSLOGIN tool. This program is usually only used in batch files and macros to find the name of the user currently logged in. You also can use this tool to get the user's configuration file or specify a new one. To use this program, follow these steps:

1. Open a command prompt. If you do not have the SourceSafe WIN32 directory in your path, change directories.
2. Enter the following command line, followed by hitting the Enter key:

        SSLOGIN -e <username> <password>

   The -e option displays the user's current project and configuration file. You may specify a different configuration file by adding the -O<filename> option.

You will rarely need to use this program from a command line. You are more likely to use this tool within a batch file to test user settings. This tool is capable of displaying a line of text with the exit code to help you determine if the program ran successfully. For more information, refer to the Visual SourceSafe Books Online.

TESTLOCK.EXE

Some networks do not support native file locking. Visual SourceSafe uses file locking for controlling access to files, especially for files that you have checked out. You only need to use this tool once to determine whether your network supports native file locking. You will only run this again if your network configuration changes. To properly test this you need two client machines capable of accessing a server with a Visual SourceSafe database. To begin the testing, follow these steps:

1. Open a command prompt on both client machines. If you do not have the SourceSafe WIN32 directory in your path, change directories.
2. Run TESTLOCK on a test folder on the server from the first client machine. You may choose any folder as long as it does not contain the TESTLOCK.EXE program. To run the program, enter the following command line, then hit the Enter key:

        TESTLOCK <path to folder on server>

3. TESTLOCK locks a file and prompts you to press any key. Without hitting a key, go to the second client machine and repeat Step 2. Your second run of TESTLOCK tries to lock the same file as the first run. If the lock fails, your network supports native file locking.

4. Press a key on both client machines to close the TESTLOCK program.

If your network does not support native file locking, the SRCSAFE.INI file for your SourceSafe database can be set to use an alternative method. By setting the Lock_Mode variable to Lockfile in the configuration file, Visual SourceSafe will avoid trying to use native locking and use the alternative method.

UNLOCK.EXE

At times, due to unexpected power or system losses, Visual SourceSafe fails to unlock certain files in the database. In that case, an error is reported when you or one of your users attempts to access a protected file. To alleviate the problem, you should use the Unlock tool to correct any problems with locked files and return them to a usable state. To use the Unlock tool, follow these steps:

1. Open a command prompt. If you do not have the SourceSafe WIN32 directory in your path, change directories.

2. Enter the following command line, followed by hitting the Enter key:

    UNLOCK <lock name>

    You must provide the lock name listed in the error message from Visual SourceSafe. This error message begins with time-out locking.

UPDINI.EXE

When you are upgrading from an older version of Visual SourceSafe, the Setup program usually updates all of your configuration files to the current format. If you have moved your configuration files from their standard location, you may need to run the UPDINI program manually. To update your old .INI files, follow these steps:

1. Open a command prompt. If you do not have the SourceSafe WIN32 directory in your path, change directories.

2. Enter the following command line, followed by hitting Enter:

    UPDINI -m<Path to your old SYSTEM.INI file>

This command line searches through the SYSTEM.INI file for each SourceSafe user and locates his or her original .INI file. It then updates each file so that your users can work with the new version. If you are looking to update a specific configuration file, follow these steps:

1. Open a command prompt. If you do not have the SourceSafe WIN32 directory in your path, change directories.

2. Enter the following command line, followed by hitting the Enter key:

```
UPDINI <Path to INI Filename>
```

Unlike the first run, this command line only updates the one configuration file if you specified the correct path.

Third-Party Utilities

Due to the nature of Visual SourceSafe, vendors other than Microsoft often have solutions for users like you. The most common third-party offerings for Visual SourceSafe are integration scripts and macros for different environments. For more information on SourceSafe options, you should refer to the Microsoft Visual SourceSafe World Wide Web site for information. Several third-party files available for free trial are included in the Free Downloads section of the SourceSafe Web site.

Microsoft Visual SourceSafe on the Web is reachable at this URL: **http://www.microsoft.com/ssafe**.

From Here...

With the dry utility information behind you, you're ready to step into the tail end of this book. Don't get misty-eyed, it's been a fun ride. From here, you can move on to:

■ Chapter 16, "Cross-Platform Usage," closes the book on a high note: peace and harmony amongst computing platforms. If your work environment involves islands of differing operating systems, Visual SourceSafe can still function fine for you. This chapter gives you the lowdown on everything you need to know.

■ Appendix A, "Batch Files and Command Line Options," continues along the command line thread by giving you sample batch files and command line summaries so you can start creating them yourself.

Cross-Platform Usage

In a perfect world, there would only be one platform. You would call this *the* platform. It would do everything for you, even walk your dog. Yes, *the* platform would make the world a better place. Moreover, it would freshen your breath while doing so. Meanwhile, while the rest of us have our heads grounded in reality, you may have the daunting task of having users of different operating systems interacting with your SourceSafe database. As much as Microsoft would like us to be all Windows, all the time, many environments are comprised of a homogenous network. Islands of Macintosh and UNIX workstations pepper the seas of Windows 95 and NT boxes. Scattered into the mix are the lowly and almost forgotten Windows for Workgroups workhorses. If this is your tale, this is your chapter. ■

More than an apple from the tree

Are you hounded by the Macintosh fanatic in your workplace? Feeling in fear of your life since you went Windows? Cast away the shackles of uncertainty and embrace SourceSafe—on a Mac!

UNIX Users Anonymous

Those who live by the command line die by UNIX. Well, perhaps not, but you UNIX developers need not be left in the cold. Visual SourceSafe for UNIX happily solves the puzzle of how to get UNIX people to use Microsoft products.

Just because you're old doesn't mean you have to be useless

Still biding time with those Windows for Workgroups workstations? Waiting for Windows 99? Well, thankfully, you don't have to throw yourself to the dogs for upgrades: there's a happy ending for Windows 3.

Apple Macintosh and MacOS

Don't let anyone tell you Microsoft doesn't love the Macintosh. If you do, you'll have a dozen of their lawyers on you quicker than you can say "System 7." Meanwhile, Microsoft itself does not produce a Macintosh version of Visual SourceSafe. This slight aside, Microsoft wisely licensed the Visual SourceSafe product for the Macintosh to development tools publisher Metrowerks. Metrowerks is widely considered one of the finest vendors for development tools for the Macintosh (as well as BeOS and the upcoming Rhapsody operating system from Apple) with its CodeWarrior environment. Its implementation of Visual SourceSafe is available under the name of Metrowerks *CodeManager*.

CodeManager is fully Visual SourceSafe 5.0 compatible and engineered for compliance to Visual SourceSafe concepts. The downside to this product is that its intended audience is programmers and developers, not Web developers specifically. The Web-oriented features of Visual SourceSafe 5.0 are not present in CodeManager at this time. CodeManager is geared toward Integrated Development Environment integration, specfically Code-Warrior. The package is available for both 68K series and PowerPC-equipped Macintosh (or MacOS-compatible) systems.

N O T E   Metrowerks on the World Wide Web is available at the following URL: **http://www. metrowerks.com**. You can reach CodeManager-specific product information at **http:// www.metrowerks.com/products/codemanager**. ▪

Marge Gets a Mac

Looking for a new machine to work on at home, Marge was suckered in by the media push for the Macintosh after the release of "Independence Day." Now that she worked at Site Corporati on a PC, she found herself wishing she could take some of her assignments home with her and work via the Site Corporati dial-up network. After pulling her back muscles picking up an MSDN shipment, she got her wish. Jose set her up with a copy of Metrowerks CodeManager and a dedicated dial-in port.

Working from home, Marge had no problem connecting to the Site Corporati local area network and the SourceSafe database. She easily checked out her work, did her thing, and checked the files back in. All this and she got to stay in bed with her PowerBook, too.

UNIX

Revision Control Systems grew out of the UNIX operating system. Like a fish to water, programmers took to RCS and the UNIX command line for their development work.

Well, there are still fish in water and developers using UNIX. With the majority of servers on the Internet using a UNIX-based operating system, many Web developers continue to use UNIX from a command line *shell*, or from the XWindow graphical user interface. While Microsoft concentrates on Visual SourceSafe for the Windows platform, licensed Visual SourceSafe to a third-party vendor named MainSoft for a UNIX implementation. The MainSoft Visual SourceSafe for UNIX product is available for several UNIX platforms: DEC, HP, IBM, SCO, SGI, and Sun.

MainSoft Visual SourceSafe for UNIX is a port of Visual SourceSafe 4.0, like Metrowerks CodeManager. The package is completely compatible with Visual SourceSafe 5.0 but does not include the Web-oriented features of the 32-bit Windows product.

> **N O T E** MainSoft on the World Wide Web is available at the following URL: **http://www.mainsoft.com**. You can reach Visual SourceSafe for UNIX-specific product information at **http://www.mainsoft.com/vssafe.htm**. ■

Jeff Digs UNIX

Jeff spent every chance he could down south to escape the cold winters in Site Corporati's hometown. Usually he would take a laptop with him and do his work, infrequently checking his e-mail and acting surly. Jeff always liked to say he couldn't update most of his work because he was connecting from a UNIX workstation. Concerned that he wasn't accomplishing enough on these "business vacations," Jose provided Jeff with MainSoft's Visual SourceSafe for UNIX. Not pleased at all with the prospect of having to do more work, Jeff plodded south in a less-than-pleasant mood.

Once down south, Jeff found no easy way to excuse his unproductive time. SourceSafe for UNIX worked flawlessly via the network. He could easily access any of his files and restore from previous versions. Jeff made a mental note to say he was using an Amiga next time.

Windows for Workgroups

Even after the hurried blitz of advertising and media exposure, many users and corporations chose to remain with good old Windows for Workgroups rather than upgrade to Windows 95. This feeling of "good enough" has left a lot of users with their (sometimes) trusty 16-bit operating system while their tools went on to brighter 32-bit pastures for Windows 95 and Windows NT. Although Microsoft Visual SourceSafe 5.0 is a 32-bit package, users of Windows for Workgroups (and Windows 3.11) can use Visual SourceSafe 4.0 to interact. As with all users of Visual SourceSafe 4.0, your 16-bit users won't be able to take advantage of SourceSafe 5.0's newer Web-oriented features, but they will be able to fully utilize SourceSafe and interact with your database.

Visual SourceSafe 4.0 includes both 32-bit and 16-bit versions of the tools. Your Windows 95 and Windows NT users should already be using SourceSafe 5.0.

> **N O T E**   Microsoft Visual SourceSafe on the World Wide Web is available at the following URL: **http://www.microsoft.com/ssafe**. Of course, if you didn't already know this you may have been sleeping through the first part of the book. ▣

Jose's Windows for Workgroups

Jose's own machine, an older PC laptop, was still running Windows for Workgroups. He simply didn't have the memory in his machine to warrant the move to Windows 95, and didn't feel it was worth buying. For his work, Windows for Workgroups did the job. Never mind the amused harassment he got from his co-workers—he was content.

That being said, Jose often went on business trips to meet with Site Corporati clients. Because he stored his own documents in the SourceSafe database, he needed an easy way to reach and modify them, while keeping the document in the Site Corporati server. Using a dial-up from a national provider, Jose connected to the Site Corporati LAN to keep up-to-date. By adding Visual SourceSafe 4.0 to his machine, Jose could then work with his SourceSafe-stored documents with ease. And seeing as he didn't really do Web design, the loss of the new Web features in version 5.0 was a minimal loss.

From Here...

With peace and harmony overflowing in your workplace, you're now ready to close this book and move on with your life. In the meantime, you may want to refer to these appendixes for more fuel in your SourceSafe journey:

- Appendix A, "Batch Files and Command Line Options," summarizes the command line facilities of Visual SourceSafe. Also for your convenience, several sample batch files that you can use for your work are included.

- Appendix B, "Visual SourceSafe Options Summary," shows you more than you ever wanted to know about the SourceSafe Explorer and Administrator Options dialog boxes. Curious about just how many options you have? Flip here.

CHAPTER 17

Epilogue

Well, the book is over and it's time to say goodbye to all those people you loved to watch grow, fight, and create. Just in case you were curious, here's what happened to your friends from Site Corporati:

Jose was offered a cushy executive position at his former place of employment, Herb's Mostly Identifiable Greasy Chicken Parts. He went on to pioneer Herb's Web presence, helping IBM perfect its matter transmission research. In 1998 he cut the ribbon on the first "Chicken Delight" ever delivered over an Internet connection.

Jeff was fired from Site Corporati after the Fliedermaus Bank of Zurich project when it was discovered he'd programmed several back doors into the Automated Teller Machine functionality. He fled to the Yukon, and for a while made a living programming the routines behind parking meters. He was last seen headed toward Mexico with a large bag of change.

Marge went on to take Jose's position after he left. She then advanced to the head of the company, and now oversees all major Web projects that Site Corporati obtains. She lives in a beach house in Trinidad with a man half her age, telling fortunes during the tourist season.

The Fliedermaus Bank of Zurich was sued by DC Comics for copyright infringement over the bank's controversial "man-bat" logo. The lawsuit crippled the bank's operating capital, and several board members resigned. The FBoZ still exists, but has given up being a traditional lending institution and has instead broken new ground in the bail bond and paycheck loan fields.

Site Corporati continued to become a force in the Web design world, signing several large clients based on the strength of its Fliedermaus Bank of Zurich project. However, the Frankenweiner project continues to create tension and sap funds from the budget to this date.

You have hopefully learned a lot more about using Visual SourceSafe in a Web setting. Remember, forewarned is forearmed. You should now have the knowledge to do just about anything you want in VSS. However, if you ever feel the urge to use your knowledge in an evil fashion, remember the lesson you learned from Jeff—he got fired and is on the run from the law. Don't let it happen to you. ●

Appendixes

Batch Files and
Command Line Options

Every now and then you get a huge stinking pile of content that is just too much to be formatted in a traditional book chapter. Luckily, long ago the Greeks invented "appendices," which means "section of the book where you put all the boring stuff." This section is not meant to replace your existing documentation, but to present a large amount of detailed information in a readable, quick-reference format. This appendix will be dealing with the bulk of the many Command Line options, and some example batch files composed of them. ∎

Command Line Summary

There are a few things you should keep in mind when entering command line comments.

Working Folder Assignments

The first thing to keep in mind is how Visual SourceSafe assigns the working folder. You can set the Command Line options as detailed in Chapter 14, "Command Line Tools," to control how the working folder is set. However, the default setting simply assumes that you want to use your current directory. The problem is, you switch to your temporary working directory and type in an SS.EXE command of some kind. You get a "bad command or file name" in response. This is because you haven't set your Visual SourceSafe executable directory as part of your system *path*. The path is set in your AUTOEXEC.BAT file, and should be edited from there. Remember that the path statement needs to point at the directory containing the executables (VSS/WIN32) and not just the VSS directory. In order to let your system know that you've changed your path, you should either run AUTOEXEC.BAT or reboot your system.

The Command Prompt

The second thing you need to remember is that all of the Command Line options must be entered from the *command prompt*. This means that you have to spawn a DOS session before being able to use Visual SourceSafe's Command Line options. You can also issue commands from the <u>R</u>un command found in the Start menu, but only in a piecemeal, one-at-a-time fashion. If you are booting into DOS mode and the Visual SourceSafe database is on another server, make sure your network settings work under DOS as well as Windows, so you can connect properly.

Prefacing Commands

Finally, all of the commands must be prefaced with ss, because this is Visual SourceSafe's command interpreter. While it would be nice to happily type things in just like DOS, it's not going to happen. All of the examples will have the requisite ss in front of them as a reminder to you. Table A.3 is a beastly, long table containing a list of VSS Command Line options, alternate wordings of those commands, and examples of how to use those commands. Every function available in the Visual SourceSafe Explorer has a command line analog. If you need a definition of a particular option, you should check your existing documentation.

Constructing a SourceSafe command line query is a simple process. The syntax is ss *<available SourceSafe commands> <available options>*. Your DOS conventions still apply to

Visual SourceSafe commands. If you want to use long file names, or names with spaces, you must enclose the text in a pair of quotation marks. All of the wild cards (*, ?) still apply. There are several flags that can modify commands and their effect on files. Most of the more universal options are presented in Table A.1. These options are appended to the end of your command string, just like any other Command Line options.

Table A.1   Parameters that Modify Command Line Options

Parameter	Function
`-C-`	No comment.
`"-CText"`	Use `Text` as the comment.
`"-C@File.TXT"`	Use the contents of `File.TXT` as the comment.
`-I-N`	Answer `No` to all questions addressed to the user.
`-I-Y`	Answer `Yes` to all questions addressed to the user.
`-NL`	Use long file names.
`-NS`	Use short file names.
`-O`	Paginate the output, with pauses inserted between pages.
`-O-`	Output only errors generated by this process.
`"-O@File.txt"`	Redirect all output to specified text file. If the file already exists, the report is appended.
`"-O&Filename"`	Redirect all error messages to specified text file. If the file already exists, the report is appended.
`-O&-`	Show no output whatsoever for this process.
`-R`	Recursive option. Forces a command to act recursively, including all of the subprojects and files in its scope.
`-Vx`	Specifies a certain file version on which to act, where applicable. The x is the desired version number, although x can also refer to a label if the label is already defined.
`-Y`	Contains user information in the form of `Username,Password`. Required for most `SS` functions.
`-?, -H`	Spawns the help listing.

There are other options available to each command line, but the previous listing covers most of the more common ones. However, you should apply common sense to your usage. For example, it's quite contradictory to use the `-c` flag on the `Comment` command. There is another command line flag that has so many options that it merits its own table: Table A.2.

The -G option determines a file's status and behavior after you've manipulated it. These options can be applied to Checkin, Checkout, Deploy, Get, Pin, Recover, Rollback, Share, Undocheckout, and Unpin operations.

Table A.2   The -G Family of Command Line Options

Command	Definition
-G-	Don't do a Get operation.
-GLpath	Copy the file to the folder specified, and not to the current or working folder.
-GTC	Add a date and time stamp to the local (working) copy.
-GTM	Add a date and time stamp from when the file was last modified.
-GTU	Add a date and time stamp from when the file was last updated.
-GCC	Compare the local copy versus the VSS database version to see if the local copy is up-to-date.
-GCK	Compare the local copy versus the VSS database version to see if the local copy is up-to-date, but using a checksum comparison method.
-GCD	As above, but using the date and time stamp to determine if the file is up-to-date.
-GR	Forces use of the carriage return character as the end-of-line character (ASCII).
-GN	Forces use of the linefeed character as the end-of-line character (UNIX).
-GRN	Forces use of a carriage return-linefeed combination as the end-of-line character (PC).
-GF	Forces the file to be moved to that project's working directory as opposed to the current directory (if the two differ).
-GF-	Turns off the effects of the –GF command, causing files to be moved to the current directory as opposed to the project's working directory.
-GWA	Activates a dialog box that queries whether you'd like to replace, skip, or merge writable files on Get and Checkout procedures.
-GWR	Replaces writable files on Get and Checkout operations.
-GWS	Skips writable files on Get and Checkout operations.
-GWM	Merges writable files on Get and Checkout operations.

The command line examples in Table A.3 are separated by a semicolon (;). You do not enter the semicolon when typing the actual command. And yes, Jose's password is actually "hello." He isn't too savvy when it comes to network security. In fact, he was hoping it would be so obvious no one would guess it. Alternate commands can replace their antecedents seamlessly.

Table A.3 Command Line Summary

Command	Alternate	Real Life Examples
About	None	SS About –YJose,hello
Add	None	SS Add Default.ASP –YJose,hello; SS Add * –R –YJose,hello
Branch	Separate	SS Branch Default.ASP –YJose,hello
Checkin	Update	SS Checkin Default.ASP –YJose,hello; SS Checkin * –R –C
Checkout	None	SS Checkout $/ –R –YJose,hello; SS Checkout Default.ASP –C
Cloak	None	SS Cloak $/Bank of Zurich/Web/Image –YJose,hello
Comment	None	SS Comment Default.ASP –V4 –YJose,hello
CP	CD, ChPro	SS CP $/Bank of Zurich/Code –YJose,hello
Create	MD, MkPro, Mp	SS Create $/Bank of Zurich/New –YJose,hello; SS Create New
Decloak	None	SS Decloak $/Bank of Zurich/Web/Image –YJose,hello
Delete	Remove	SS Delete $/Bank of Zurich –YJose,hello; SS Delete Default.ASP
Deploy	None	SS Deploy $/ –R –YJose,hello; SS Deploy Default.ASP –V3
Destroy	None	SS Destroy $/ –R –I- –YJose,hello; SS Destroy Default.ASP
Diff	None	SS Diff $/Bank of Zurich/Web –YJose,hello; SS Diff Default.ASP
Directory	Dir, LS	SS Dir $/ –R –YJose,hello; SS Dir $/Bank of Zurich –O@Report.txt
Filetype	None	SS Filetype Default.ASP;
FindInFiles	Scan, Grep	SS FindInFiles "tutti frutti" Default.ASP –YJose,hello
Get	None	SS Get $/Bank of Zurich/Web –R –YJose,hello; SS Get *.ASP

continues

Table A.3 Continued

Command	Alternate	Real Life Examples
Help	None	SS Help -YJose,hello; SS Help Filetype -YJose,hello
History	None	SS History $/Bank of Zurich -YJose,hello; SS History Default.ASP -O
Label	None	SS Label Default.ASP -V2 -YJose,hello
Locate	WhereIs	SS Locate Default.ASP -YJose,hello
Links	None	SS Links Default.ASP -YJose,hello
Merge	None	SS Merge $/Bank of Zurich/Web-O@mergereport.txt -YJose,hello
Move	None	SS Move $/Bank of Zurich/Web $/ Bank of Zurich/Miscellaneous
Password	None	SS Password
Paths	None	SS Paths Default.ASP -YJose,hello
Pin	None	SS Pin Default.ASP -V3 -YJose,hello; SS Pin *.HTM -VLive
Project	None	SS Project -YJose,hello;
Properties	None	SS Properties Default.ASP -YJose,hello; SS Properties $/Web
Purge	None	SS Purge Default.ASP -YJose,hello; SS Purge $/Bank of Zurich
Recover	Undelete	SS Recover Default.ASP -YJose,hello; SS Recover $/Bank of Zurich
Rename	None	SS Rename Default.ASP Default.OLD -YJose,hello
Rollback	None	SS Rollback Default.ASP -V15 -YJose,hello;
Share	None	SS Share Default.ASP -YJose,hello; SS Share $/Bank of Zurich
Status	None	SS Status $/Bank of Zurich -YJose,hello; SS Status Default.ASP
UndoCheckout	Uncheckout	SS UndoCheckout Default.ASP -YJose,hello;

Command	Alternate	Real Life Examples
Unpin	None	SS Unpin Default.ASP -YJose,hello; SS Unpin $/Web/*.DOC
View	Type	SS View Default.ASP -YJose,hello
WhoAmI	None	SS WhoAmI -YJose,hello
WorkFold	None	SS WorkFold $/Bank of Zurich/Web C:\Temp -YJose,hello
YNC	None	SS YNC $/Bank of Zurich/Web -YJose,hello

Most of the previous commands can work on either a project or a file. The -Y flag is required for *every* command, all the way down to the trivial About command. The -Y is often left off the end of second examples in the interests of brevity. You can enter commands without -Y, but you have to enter your account information and password anyway. Note that not every possible command line option was explored, as there are several command-specific flags. Once again, this listing is just a handy reference guide and is not meant to replace your software documentation.

Sample Batch Files

All the great masters stole their work and ideas from those who came before. Leonardo Da Vinci, Michaelangelo, Jan Von Eyck—all are derivatives of a cave painter named Zog. Hopefully, these sample batch files can serve as your inspiration as well, so steal away.

Before you get all excited about creating batch files, there are some things to keep mind. First of all, you should have a -I argument attached to any batch you create, so you don't get extraneous interactivity clogging up your procedure. You should also remember to always include the -Y information, because a user information request will stall your batch faster than you can say "antiestablishmentarianism." The following sample batch files can extend basic Visual SourceSafe functionality to nearly any development platform that allows you to define external commands.

The first example is that of a check in. A check out would be exactly the same file, except that the requisite command would be different. Batch files can accept command line parameters; they store them in placeholder variables called %1, %2, and so on. When you see a %1 in the file, you know that it means the first Command Line option that came after the executable. That is essentially the extent of the knowledge required to create a batch file.

Listing A.1   CHECKIN.BAT—A Simple Batch File Allowing the Check In of up to Nine Files.

```
@ECHO OFF
REM Checkin.bat created March 10/97 as an example for
REM Web Management with Microsoft Visual SourceSafe
REM Example borrows heavily from online documentation
REM -Chris Denschikoff

SS checkin -O- -C- -I-Y %1 %2 %3 %4 %5 %6 %7 %8 %9 -YJose,hello
IF errorlevel 100 GOTO AB_TERMINATION

REM Exit code 0, File successfully checked in
ECHO File was successfully checked back in.
GOTO END

rem Exit code 100, abnormal termination
:AB_TERMINATION
ECHO Visual SourceSafe could not initialize, let alone execute your command.
ECHO This is probably because the file isn't checked out in the first place.

:END
```

Notice in Listing A.1 the use of the -O- flag to eliminate all output, the -Y flag to register the user, the -I-Y flag to answer Yes to all questions, and the -C- flag to eliminate any comment associated with the process. When Visual SourceSafe runs, it will generate an *exit code* as it terminates. This exit code tells you how and why the program stopped processing. An exit code of 0 means a successful run. The exit code of 100 means something went disastrously wrong, and an exit code of 1 (not shown) means something went wrong but that SourceSafe still managed to run. The error code of 1 only occurs in three different instances. The first is when you enter a Status command and there is at least one file checked out. The second is when you enter a Directory command, yet there are no files in the project to be listed, and the last is when you make a Diff call, and there is at least one difference between the two files. If you want to use the exit code of 1 for trapping purposes, those are the only three circumstances in which it will arise.

N O T E   This isn't a tutorial about "How to Make Batch Files for MS-DOS Platforms," it's only an introduction to some of the concepts you'll need. Refer to your operating system's documentation for the exact requirements on creating batch files and scripts. ■

The next example is of an Add function extended to a batch file. You would use this in conjunction with any editing software in which you are creating files and need to have them added to the Visual SourceSafe database quickly. Note the similarities in Listing A.2 to the previous listing, Listing A.1.

Listing A.2   ADD.BAT—Using Batch Extensibility Can Add the Functionality of Visual SourceSafe to Programs that Wouldn't Necessarily Have It

```
@ECHO OFF
REM Add.bat created March 10/97 as an example for
REM Web Management with Microsoft Visual SourceSafe
REM Example borrows heavily from online documentation
REM -Chris Denschikoff

SS Add -O- -C- -I-Y %1 %2 %3 %4 %5 %6 %7 %8 %9 -YJose,hello
if errorlevel 100 goto AB_TERMINATION

REM Exit code 0, File successfully added.
ECHO File was successfully added.
goto END

rem Exit code 100, abnormal termination
:AB_TERMINATION
ECHO Visual SourceSafe could not initialize, let alone execute your command.
ECHO This is probably because the file already exists in the project, or it
ECHO doesn't exist on your local drive.

:END
```

Visual SourceSafe Options Summary

Both the Visual SourceSafe Explorer and Visual
SourceSafe Administrator provide you with a number
of options for configuration. The Options dialog boxes
for both programs share some similarities, but they're
not quite long, lost twins. Each program's scope differs.
The goal of this appendix is to provide you with a complete breakdown of each of the options in the dialog
boxes and what each of those options does. ■

Visual SourceSafe Explorer

The SourceSafe Explorer's Options dialog box is divided into eight individual tabs. Each of these tabs reflects a particular aspect of Visual SourceSafe's operations. Each of the tabs is discussed in detail here. You can open the Options dialog box by choosing Tools, Options.

General

The General tab in Figure B.1 is usable by any SourceSafe user. It does not require special permissions.

FIG. B.1
The General tab is used to control the overall behavior of certain SourceSafe features.

- Always Keep Files Checked Out. This option keeps a copy of your file checked out in your working directory, even after you have checked the file back in. You may use this to update the database with your changes while continuing to modify the file.

- Act on Projects Recursively. By choosing this option, you force SourceSafe to recursively act on projects for actions. This means the selected project as well as any subprojects are affected by your actions.

- Reuse Last Comment. In the event that you want to apply the same comment to several files you are checking in, this option carries over your previous comments to each file. If you modify the comment in the comment box, the next file will use your new comment.

- Check In Unchanged Files. This drop box sets how Visual SourceSafe should treat files that are checked in without any changes. By default, SourceSafe carries out an undocheckout. You can configure this to prompt you for instructions, check the file in regardless, or undo the check out.

- Use <u>V</u>isual Merge. When you are dealing with multiple check ins, the changes must be merged into one final document. You can specify how Visual SourceSafe will act during this merge with this drop box: Yes, Use Visual Merge; No, Use Manual Merge; or Use Visual Merge Only if there are conflicts.

- <u>D</u>ouble-Click a File. Using this drop box, you can specify how Visual SourceSafe should determine its behavior when you double-click a file in the SourceSafe Explorer. The options are: Ask what to do; View the file using the associated viewer; or Edit the file using the associated editor. Holding the Shift key while double-clicking a file will override any of these settings and instead use the Ask option.

- <u>E</u>ditor for Viewing Files. Using the <u>B</u>rowse button or by manually entering the path, you can choose the editor to use for viewing files. You launch this program when you select the View command.

- Folder for <u>T</u>emporary Files. By default, Visual SourceSafe uses a directory named TEMP in the same folder as your SRCSAFE.INI to store its temporary files. You may use the Bro<u>w</u>se button or manually enter the path for an alternate directory.

Local Files

The Local Files tab in Figure B.2 is usable by any SourceSafe user. It does not require special permissions.

FIG. B.2
The Local Files tab sets the behavior of local copies in your working directory.

- Remove Local Copy After <u>A</u>dd or Check In. With this option selected, Visual SourceSafe always deletes the local working copy of a file when you check the file in or add it to the database. Use this as a means for conservation of disk space. This is also your guarantee that you are working with the latest version of a document in your working directory.

- ■ Remove Local Copy After Delete. This automatically deletes the local working copy of a file when you choose to delete it from the database. You can recover this file as long as you have not destroyed the file or purged the project.

- ■ Use Read-Only Flag for Files that Are not Checked Out. Using this option sets the read-only flag for your working directory files. You are only able to edit files you have checked out. Knowing that you have not been modifying files that are not checked out is used as a means of identification for SourceSafe.

- ■ Copy Keyword-Expanded Files into Working Folder. When you are using keywords in your files, Visual SourceSafe replaces information each time you check a file in. With this option, SourceSafe always copies the checked in file back to the working directory to make sure the working copy is up-to-date. This adds to performance overhead.

- ■ Append End-of-Line to All Text Files. If your files do not have an end-of-line character present, this option adds one to each line that needs it. This is typically used for compilers, and is rarely required for Web pages.

- ■ Compare Files By. This option determines how Visual SourceSafe detects a file that has been changed when you check it into the database. The drop box offers three methods: Contents, Checksum, and Time. Determination by contents is the most reliable but also the slowest. SourceSafe compares the full contents of the working file to the copy in the database to determine if a change has occurred. Checksum compares by a checksum stored within the SourceSafe database. Finally, Time compares the date and time flags for the file.

- ■ Replace Writable Files. On any action that copies a file to your working directory (GET or check out), Visual SourceSafe replaces documents of the same name. This option determines how SourceSafe should handle replacing documents that are not read-only and potentially modified files. The drop box offers four options: Ask, to give you the option each time; Replace, to replace the file regardless of read-only or not; Skip, to abort replacing the writable file; and Merge, to merge the changes between the checked out file and the writable copy in your working directory.

- ■ Set Date/Time on Local Files. This option controls how Visual SourceSafe affixes the date and time stamp on your files. By default, when you check out or GET a file, Visual SourceSafe uses the current date and time for the stamp. Using the drop box, you can change this behavior to use the date/time that the file was modified (Modification), or to use the date/time that the file was checked in (Check In).

View

The View tab in Figure B.3 is usable by any SourceSafe user. It does not require special permissions.

FIG. B.3

The View tab controls how you view information within the SourceSafe Explorer.

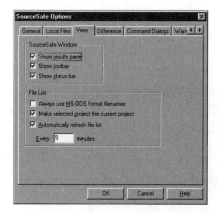

- ■ Show Results Pane. When selected, this option shows the bottom pane of the Visual SourceSafe Explorer window. The results pane shows you the results of your actions in Visual SourceSafe.

- ■ Show Toolbar. When selected, this option displays the toolbar below the menu bar for SourceSafe Explorer. The toolbar contains several *butcons* (button icons) that act as shortcuts for actions in SourceSafe.

- ■ Show Status Bar. When selected, this option displays the status bar at the bottom of the SourceSafe Explorer window. The status bar contains information such as the current username, the current sort order for file lists, and the number of files in the list.

- ■ Always Use MS-DOS Format Filenames. If you are working with platforms that do not support long file names, such as Windows for Workgroups, enabling this option truncates long file names to the standard 8.3 MS-DOS format.

- ■ Make Selected Project the Current Project. By default, when you select a project from the project list, the file list updates accordingly. If you want to speed up your use of Explorer, especially if you're working on a slow network, you may want to disable this option. With this option disabled you must double-click a project to update the file list to the selected project.

- ■ Automatically Refresh File List. With this option selected, Visual SourceSafe automatically updates the file list periodically. Below the check box is a text box in which you can specify the number of minutes between refreshes. With this option enabled, you may experience momentary slowdowns as the file updates. If you do not have this option enabled, you must manually update the file list by choosing View, Refresh File List from the menu bar.

Difference

The Difference tab in Figure B.4 is usable by any SourceSafe user. It does not require special permissions.

FIG. B.4

The Difference tab lets you customize your differences dialog box display. Setting custom fonts and colors makes your work easier.

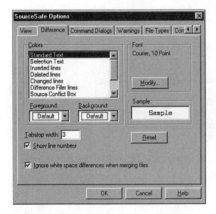

- ■ Colors. The colors list box lets you customize the foreground and background colors for the different dialog boxes in Visual SourceSafe, including the Differences and Merge dialogs. The list contains 10 styles that you may assign unique colors.

- ■ Font. Using the Modify button, you may set the default font style and size for viewer windows.

- ■ Tabstop Width. By default, the viewer windows use three spaces to represent a tab. You may change the size of a tab by modifying the text box.

- ■ Show Line Numbers. With this option selected, Visual SourceSafe viewer windows display line numbers.

- ■ Ignore White Space Differences when Merging Files. When you select this option, Visual SourceSafe ignores tabs and spaces for merging.

- ■ Reset. By clicking this button, all values on this tab are reset to their default values.

Command Dialogs

The Command Dialogs tab in Figure B.5 is usable by any SourceSafe user. It does not require special permissions.

FIG. B.5
The Command
Dialogs tab lets you
determine if you want
to see command
dialogs for certain
actions.

■ Display Dialog Box when These Commands Are Used on a File. By using the check boxes, you may choose to have the command dialog box appear when you carry out an action on a file. If you never use the options in the dialog box, you may choose to disable the Command Dialogs entirely.

■ Display Dialog Box when These Commands Are Used on a Project. Much like with a file, you may select to have the command dialog box appear when you carry out an action on a project. If you never use the options in the dialog box, you may choose to disable the Command Dialogs entirely.

Each option represents a particular SourceSafe action, such as Get Latest Version and Check Out.

Warnings

The Warnings tab in Figure B.6 is usable by any SourceSafe user. It does not require special permissions.

FIG. B.6
The Warnings
tab allows you to
customize warnings
in the SourceSafe
Explorer.

■ Display Warning for These Commands. Each of the check boxes represents an action that involves warning dialog boxes. With the option selected, you must confirm the warning before your action completes. If you do not have the option selected, there is no warning when you carry out the action.

File Types

The File Types tab in Figure B.7 is usable by any SourceSafe user. It does not require special permissions.

FIG. B.7
The File Types tab, discussed in detail in Chapter 12, lets you set file type groups for SourceSafe Explorer.

■ Binary Files. The text box may contain comma-separated file extensions for file types that SourceSafe should automatically consider binary files. This overrides SourceSafe's detection of file types when you check files in.

■ Create SCC File. This text box lets you specify a comma-separated list of file extensions to have SCC files created. You may use the SCC file for some development environments and compilers.

■ File Groups. The list box contains the defined file type groups for Visual SourceSafe. Clicking the Add button lets you add a new file group to the list. You can find instructions for adding file types in Chapter 12, "Visual SourceSafe Administration." You may remove an existing file type group by selecting the group and clicking the Delete button.

■ File Types Included in the File Group. By selecting a file group from the list box you can see the extensions of related file types in this text box. A comma separates each file type extension.

Command Line Options

The Command Line Options tab in Figure B.8 is usable by any SourceSafe user. It does not require special permissions.

FIG. B.8
The Command Line Options tab is used to customize Source-Safe's behavior at a command line.

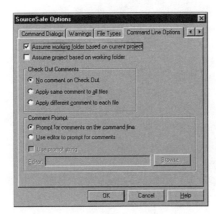

- Assume Working Folder Based on Current Project. If this option is set, Visual SourceSafe uses the working folder set for the current project with which you are working. All files that you check out automatically get copied into the working folder, regardless of where you are located in the command line.

- Assume Project Based on Working Folder. If this option is set, Visual SourceSafe uses the current directory you are in as the means of determining what project you are using. If you check in a file from a directory that is the working directory for a certain project, you automatically switch to that project without having to manually do so.

- Check Out Comments. Using the radio button set, you may control how comments are applied to your check outs. By default, you use the No Comment option and do not enter a comment. You may choose to use the same comment for all files, or apply a unique comment to each file.

- Comment Prompt. You may choose to enter your SourceSafe comments from the command line or from an external editor. If you choose to use an external editor, you must define the path to the editor.

Visual SourceSafe Administrator

The SourceSafe Administrator's Options dialog box is divvied into six individual tabs. Each of these tabs controls your SourceSafe installation. Each of the tabs is discussed in detail here. You can open the Options dialog box by choosing Tools, Options.

General

The General tab in Figure B.9 is usable only by the Administrator.

FIG. B.9
The General tab
controls simple
aspects of your
SourceSafe
installation.

- Allow <u>M</u>ultiple Checkouts. Normally only one user may check out a file at a time. You may choose to allow more than one of your users to check out a file at a time. The first person to check the file in updates the database and each subsequent check in merges the changes.

    ▶ To find out more about the simultaneous checking-in of updated files, **see** Chapter 9, "Working in Teams," **p. 119.**

- Use <u>N</u>etwork Name for Automatic User Log In. In using this option, users do not need to enter a username and password at a dialog box before using SourceSafe. If the users' names are not the same as their Windows networking usernames, you do not need to select this option.

- <u>D</u>atabase Name. By default your database has no unique name, other than its path. If you're often dealing with different databases you may want to assign a name to it. The name of the database appears in the title bar of the SourceSafe Explorer.

- E<u>x</u>pand Keywords in Files of this Type. By default, Visual SourceSafe does not expand the keywords inside files when you check them in or add them. File types that have their extensions listed in this text box (separated by a comma) will have their keywords expanded.

- <u>L</u>og all Actions in a Journal File. If you're interested in keeping track of when your users are modifying your database, you may choose to keep a journal. By entering a path in this text box, all actions that affect data appear in the journal. Actions that do not modify the database do not appear.

Project Security

The Project Security tab in Figure B.10 is usable only by the Administrator.

FIG. B.10
The Project Security tab defines the access rights for your SourceSafe database.

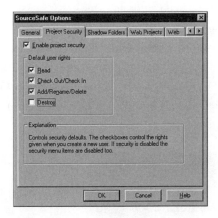

Part

V

App

B

- Enable Project Security. By selecting this option you are informing Visual SourceSafe that you want to use access rights and security for your database. Once you have selected this option, you should use the check boxes below it to set your default access rights. All rights have a direct correlation on one another.

- Read. Your user can see the contents of a project and view files.

- Check Out/Check In. Your user can freely check a file out of the database, carry out changes, and then update the database with the modifications.

- Add/Rename/Delete. Your user can freely add new files to a project as well as delete files from a project. Your user is also able to rename files in a project.

- Destroy. Your user can destroy files, purge files and projects, and carry out destructive operations such as rollback.

Shadow Folders

The Shadow Folders tab in Figure B.11 is usable only by the Administrator.

- Set Shadow Folder for Project. Specifies the path for your SourceSafe project. You may also use the Browse button to select the project.

- Set Shadow Folder To. Specifies the destination path for your shadow folder. This is where your project files arrive. You may use the Browse button to select the path.

- Set Read-Only Flag for all Files. With this option selected, Visual SourceSafe sets all files copied into the shadow folder as read-only.

- ■ <u>E</u>nd-of-Line Character for Files. This drop box specifies the end-of-line character for your files. This is usually of importance to programmers and certain compilers. By default, this is a combination of a carriage return (CR) and a line feed (LF). You may choose to use only a carriage return or line feed.

- ■ <u>F</u>ile Date/Time. You can set how Visual SourceSafe should set the time and date stamp for files copied into the shadow folder by using this drop box. By default, this is the current date and time. You may choose to use the time/date on which the file was modified, or the time/date at which the file was checked into the database.

- ■ Set <u>A</u>nother. By clicking this button you commit your changes to the database and can specify a new shadow folder.

FIG. B.11

The Shadow Folders tab is used to define and control your projects' shadow folders.

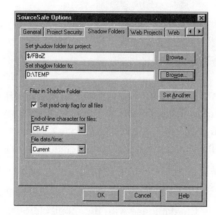

Web Projects

The Web Projects tab in Figure B.12 is usable only by the Administrator.

FIG. B.12

The Web Projects tab lets you specify your Web Projects settings.

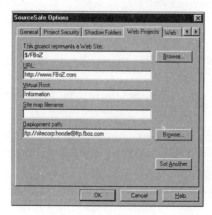

- This Project Represents a Web Site. Use this text box to enter your Visual SourceSafe project path. You may also use the Browse button to select your project.

- URL. Enter your Web site's address, or URL, in this text box. You do not need to specify the subdirectory in this text box.

- Virtual Root. If your Web site is a subdirectory from a Web server, enter the subdirectory here. Do not enter the preceding slash.

- Site Map Filename. By default, Visual SourceSafe site maps are named SITEMAP.HTM. You may choose to change the name of this file with this text box.

- Deployment Path. Enter your Web site's publishing path in this text box. You may enter a local directory or LAN path, or an FTP URL. If you need to specify a username and password for an FTP path, enter it in the following format: ftp:// username:password@ftp.servername.dom. You may use the Browse button to set a local or LAN directory path.

- Set Another. By clicking this button you commit your changes to the database and can define a new Web Project.

Web

The Web tab in Figure B.13 is usable only by the Administrator.

FIG. B.13
The Web tab defines the behavior for Visual SourceSafe's Web deployment features.

- Proxy for Deploying Over FTP. If you are working behind a corporate firewall or proxy server, you may need to specify proxy information. If you do not specify your proxy server, you may not be able to publish to a server on the Internet using FTP. Enter the address for your proxy server in this text box, usually with the numbered IP address.

- ■ <u>D</u>o Not Use the Proxy for These Local Servers. If you are also deploying content to servers behind your firewall, you should enter their numbered IP addresses in this text box, separated by a comma. This prevents Visual SourceSafe from trying to go through the proxy server to publish to these machines.

- ■ Default <u>F</u>ilename for Web Pages. For Visual SourceSafe's hyperlink verification process, you should enter the default file name for Web pages in this text box. This file name defaults to DEFAULT.HTM.

File Types

The File Types tab in Figure B.14 is usable only by the Administrator.

FIG. B.14

The File Types tab in the SourceSafe Administrator is identical to that of the SourceSafe Explorer, except that it affects all users.

- ■ <u>B</u>inary Files. The text box may contain comma-separated file extensions for file types that SourceSafe should automatically consider binary files. This overrides SourceSafe's detection of file types when you check files in.

- ■ <u>F</u>ile Groups. The list box contains the defined file type groups for Visual SourceSafe. Clicking the <u>A</u>dd button lets you add a new file group to the list. You can find instructions for adding file types in Chapter 12, "Visual SourceSafe Administration." You may remove an existing file type group by selecting the group and clicking the <u>D</u>elete button.

- ■ File <u>T</u>ypes Included in File Group. By selecting a file group from the list box you can see the extensions of related file types in this text box. A comma separates each file type extension.

- ■ <u>C</u>reate SCC File. This text box lets you specify a comma-separated list of file extensions to have SCC files created. You may use the SCC file for some development environments and compilers.

Index

X-Y-Z

Complete and Return this Card
for a *FREE* Computer Book Catalog

Thank you for purchasing this book! You have purchased a superior computer book written expressly for your needs. To continue to provide the kind of up-to-date, pertinent coverage you've come to expect from us, we need to hear from you. Please take a minute to complete and return this self-addressed, postage-paid form. In return, we'll send you a free catalog of all our computer books on topics ranging from word processing to programming and the internet.

Mr. ☐   Mrs. ☐   Ms. ☐   Dr. ☐

Name (first) ☐☐☐☐☐☐☐☐☐☐☐   (M.I.) ☐   (last) ☐☐☐☐☐☐☐☐☐☐☐☐☐☐☐

Address ☐☐☐☐☐☐☐☐☐☐☐☐☐☐☐☐☐☐☐☐☐☐☐☐☐☐☐☐☐☐
☐☐☐☐☐☐☐☐☐☐☐☐☐☐☐☐☐☐☐☐☐☐☐☐☐☐☐☐☐☐

City ☐☐☐☐☐☐☐☐☐☐☐☐☐☐   State ☐☐   Zip ☐☐☐☐☐☐☐☐☐

Phone ☐☐☐ ☐☐☐ ☐☐☐☐   Fax ☐☐☐ ☐☐☐ ☐☐☐☐

Company Name ☐☐☐☐☐☐☐☐☐☐☐☐☐☐☐☐☐☐☐☐☐☐☐☐☐☐☐

E-mail address ☐☐☐☐☐☐☐☐☐☐☐☐☐☐☐☐☐☐☐☐☐☐☐☐☐☐☐

Please check at least (3) influencing factors for purchasing this book.

Front or back cover information on book .... ☐
Special approach to the content .... ☐
Completeness of content .... ☐
Author's reputation .... ☐
Publisher's reputation .... ☐
Book cover design or layout .... ☐
Index or table of contents of book .... ☐
Price of book .... ☐
Special effects, graphics, illustrations .... ☐
Other (Please specify): _____ ☐

How did you first learn about this book?

Saw in Macmillan Computer Publishing catalog .... ☐
Recommended by store personnel .... ☐
Saw the book on bookshelf at store .... ☐
Recommended by a friend .... ☐
Received advertisement in the mail .... ☐
Saw an advertisement in: _____ ☐
Read book review in: _____ ☐
Other (Please specify): _____ ☐

How many computer books have you purchased in the last six months?

This book only .... ☐   3 to 5 books .... ☐
Books .... ☐   More than 5 .... ☐

4. Where did you purchase this book?

Bookstore .... ☐
Computer Store .... ☐
Consumer Electronics Store .... ☐
Department Store .... ☐
Office Club .... ☐
Warehouse Club .... ☐
Mail Order .... ☐
Direct from Publisher .... ☐
Internet site .... ☐
Other (Please specify): _____ ☐

5. How long have you been using a computer?

☐ Less than 6 months   ☐ 6 months to a year
☐ 1 to 3 years   ☐ More than 3 years

6. What is your level of experience with personal computers and with the subject of this book?

	With PCs	With subject of book
New	☐	☐
Casual	☐	☐
Accomplished	☐	☐
Expert	☐	☐

Source Code ISBN: 0-7897-1233-4

7. Which of the following best describes your job title?

Administrative Assistant .... ☐
Coordinator .... ☐
Manager/Supervisor .... ☐
Director .... ☐
Vice President .... ☐
President/CEO/COO .... ☐
Lawyer/Doctor/Medical Professional .... ☐
Teacher/Educator/Trainer .... ☐
Engineer/Technician .... ☐
Consultant .... ☐
Not employed/Student/Retired .... ☐
Other (Please specify): _____ ☐

8. Which of the following best describes the area of the company your job title falls under?

Accounting .... ☐
Engineering .... ☐
Manufacturing .... ☐
Operations .... ☐
Marketing .... ☐
Sales .... ☐
Other (Please specify): _____ ☐

Comments: _____
_____
_____

9. What is your age?

Under 20 .... ☐
21-29 .... ☐
30-39 .... ☐
40-49 .... ☐
50-59 .... ☐
60-over .... ☐

10. Are you:

Male .... ☐
Female .... ☐

11. Which computer publications do you read regularly? (Please list)

_____
_____
_____
_____
_____
_____
_____
_____
_____
_____

Fold here and scotch-tape to ma

Check out Que® Books on the World Wide Web
http://www.quecorp.com

As the biggest software release in computer history, Windows 95 continues to redefine the computer industry. Click here for the latest info on our Windows 95 books

Make computing quick and easy with these products designed exclusively for new and casual users

Examine the latest releases in word processing, spreadsheets, operating systems, and suites

The Internet, The World Wide Web, CompuServe®, America Online®, Prodigy® —it's a world of ever-changing information. Don't get left behind!

Find out about new additions to our site, new bestsellers and hot topics

In-depth information on high-end topics: find the best reference books for databases, programming, networking, and client/server technologies

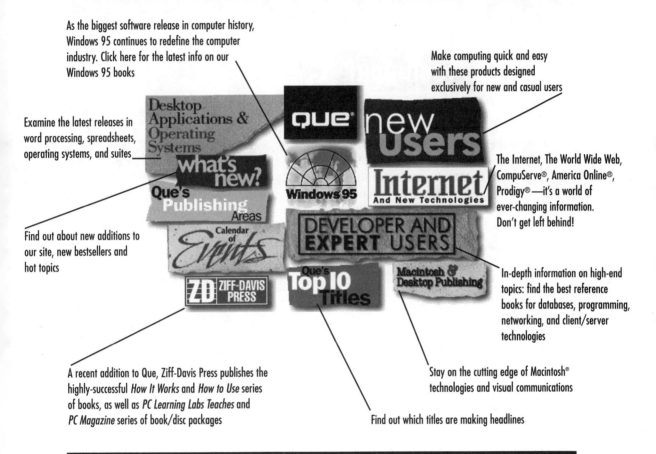

A recent addition to Que, Ziff-Davis Press publishes the highly-successful *How It Works* and *How to Use* series of books, as well as *PC Learning Labs Teaches* and *PC Magazine* series of book/disc packages

Stay on the cutting edge of Macintosh® technologies and visual communications

Find out which titles are making headlines

With 6 separate publishing groups, Que develops products for many specific market segments and areas of computer technology. Explore our Web Site and you'll find information on best-selling titles, newly published titles, upcoming products, authors, and much more.

- Stay informed on the latest industry trends and products available
- Visit our online bookstore for the latest information and editions
- Download software from Que's library of the best shareware and freeware

MACMILLAN COMPUTER PUBLISHING USA

A VIACOM COMPANY

Technical ---- Support:

If you need assistance with the information in this book or with a CD/Disk accompanying the book, please access the Knowledge Base on our Web site at **http://www.superlibrary.com/general/support**. Our most Frequently Asked Questions are answered there. If you do not find the answer to your questions on our Web site, you may contact Macmillan Technical Support **(317) 581-3833** or e-mail us at **support@mcp.com**.